They Never Rationed Courage

LETTERS HOME FROM THE WAR

1940 – 1945

ALSO BY TOM PATTERSON

First Stage: The Making of the Stratford Festival

THEY NEVER
RATIONED COURAGE

LETTERS HOME FROM THE WAR

1940 – 1945

TOM PATTERSON

THE MERCURY PRESS

The publisher gratefully acknowledges the financial assistance of the Canada Council and the Ontario Arts Council, as well as that of the Government of Ontario through the Ontario Publishing Centre.

Edited by Beverley Daurio
Cover design by TASK
Composition and book design by TASK

Cover photograph, from right to left: "Gabby" Gautier, Tom Patterson, "J.J." McDonald, Alec McNeil, with Muriel Stamp; spine photo: Tom Patterson; page one photo, from left to right: Captain Bill Hamilton, an unknown Captain, Sergeant Tom Patterson, Sergeant Fred Church, Private Leslie Tasker; title page photo: Tom Patterson with Muriel Stamp

Printed and bound in Canada by Metropole Litho
Printed on acid-free paper
First Edition
1 2 3 4 5 99 98 97 96 95

Canadian Cataloguing in Publication Data

Patterson, Tom, 1920-
They never rationed courage : letters home from the War, 1940 - 45
ISBN 1-55128-026-4
1. Patterson, Tom, 1920-   . 2. World War, 1939-1945 - Personal narratives, Canadian.
I. Title.
D811.P3   940.54'8171   C95-932332-5

Represented in Canada by the Literary Press Group
Distributed in Canada by General Distribution Services

The Mercury Press
137 Birmingham Street
Stratford, Ontario
Canada   N5A 2T1

Dedicated to Festival archivist Lisa Brant
without whose inquiring mind and enthusiasm
this book would never have come to be.

— 1940 —

June 4

Dear Mom and Dad,

We are leaving at 7:20 tonight. I may not be able to write again until we get across the ocean; I thought I'd better let you know that.

Everybody is getting packed; we could almost be taking a trip to camp. Things really went smoothly when we left, didn't they? I am glad it was that way. It helps a lot.

The weather here has been sweltering— about 82°— and it's a son-of-a-gun in these uniforms. I'd better get this posted— I haven't too much time.

So long, and love,
Tom

June 10

Dear Mom and Dad,

We *can* send mail, but it will be censored.

We left London, Ontario, late on Tuesday; after riding all night, we arrived in Ottawa Wednesday morning. Captain Grayson was orderly officer and I was orderly Sergeant. We did all right, I think, considering it was our first time.

The Dental Corps are a swell bunch of fellows and the Sergeant I am with is a peach. We are all happy, well fed, and being treated like kings. Here is a menu from yesterday:

DINNER

Vegetable Soup

Baked Stuffed Haddock, Sauce Piquante

Canadian Pot Roast Beef

Green Peas

Mashed Potatoes

Steamed Jam Roll Pudding

Coffee

The one Frenchman with us can't speak any English. He was pretty blue at first, but is cheering up now.

I'd better hurry. Give my best to all the folks and excuse the writing; I am standing up to write this.

Love,

Tom

June 21

Dear Mom and Dad,

Last Monday night in London, the Headquarters of the Dental Corps gave us a good party and I met a lot of swell fellows. The people on the train to Ottawa were kind to the 10 of us travelling together and made our trip quite nice. In Ottawa on Wednesday we were given leave in the afternoon. First we went to the top of the Peace Tower, then, because we are soldiers, the Mounties allowed us into the House of Commons. At 3:00 p.m., the House went into session. We saw the Speaker's parade, I met Fred Sanderson [Perth County's M.P.], and we got seats in the Members' Gallery; we were only there long enough to see the Liberals boo down Dr. Bruce.

I think the Landsdowne Park barracks is the worst in Canada.

On Thursday we were all Confined to Barracks (C.B.'d) and I was orderly Sergeant and Captain Grayson was orderly officer. We had quite a day, going through the gas room and getting a taste of tear gas. Some stuff. Then we drew all our web equipment and were a very tired bunch when we went to bed.

Friday morning we paraded down to the station after General Odlum took the salute. The Dental Corps are sure a straggly bunch when it comes to marching! Then we pulled out on the best train trip I have ever had.

We were in a Colony Car; it was plenty dirty, but not much worse than some I've travelled in to Toronto. We missed Montreal; the first city we came to was Quebec. The thing that got me was the way the French people acted. Everybody from Quebec City to Halifax and within 10 miles of the railway stations knew we were coming. If anybody tries to tell you that the French are unloyal, shoot him, with my compliments. Farmers all along the way came out to wave us goodbye. In Quebec, where a lot of the soldiers are from, women were carrying red, white, and blue fruit baskets, with Union Jacks sticking out of the fruit.

We took a 15-minute route march to stretch our legs, and that was the last time we were off the train till we got to Halifax. We crossed the St. Lawrence over the Quebec Bridge and came into Charni— a little village about the size of Sebringville. They had a policeman there to keep the crowd back, it was so big; they weren't all kids, either. Young girls, old men, women, and young boys came running, jumping fences and anything else that got in their way. None of them could speak much English, and they told us to talk slower.

The Frenchman with us who couldn't speak English had a field day with the people in Quebec, but I felt sorry for him at times—

he couldn't enter into the fun on the train. Then we came into Riviere de Loup, a city of 10,000 south of the St. Lawrence. They had even had bleachers built, and about 8,000 people came to see us. None of them could speak English; there were 12 English families in the whole place. The cheering crowds made a sight I can't describe, and we will probably never see the like again. As we passed through farming areas, the people stopped work in the fields to watch us. In one little place of about 100 people we stopped to take on water. On the station platform were a few people, and in front of them a wizened up old priest with his prayerbook. By this time, it was getting dark, and in every village and town we went through, people looked out their windows at us and the station platforms were packed.

At Grand Falls in New Brunswick, a mob greeted us, and the I.O.D.E. gave us cigarettes and magazines. As the train pulled out we gave three cheers for the I.O.D.E. This kind of thing happened all the way along the line and got even better as we went east. We arrived in Halifax Saturday afternoon and after much red tape got on the boat. Sergeant Poole from London, a Sergeant Murphy from Ottawa, and Sergeant McNeil from Toronto are in the same cabin with me on B deck, and it is very nice. After unpacking and washing, we took a stroll around the boat, the Duchess of Bedford. The crew and stewards are good to us. Docked behind us was the Revenge, unloading gold bullion from Britain. It is really a powerful looking thing, and is the crew ever smart. We stayed in dock until Tuesday morning, June 11. Some birthday present, eh!

At eight o'clock Tuesday morning, we watched the ceremony of the raising of the flag on the Revenge, with everybody in full dress uniform and the band out. This takes place every morning while in dock. Each group marches and makes a three-sided square formation, with the flag filling in the fourth side. The band plays "God Save the King" as the flag is rising, and all the officers salute. They have it timed so perfectly that the flag reaches the top of the pole on the last note.

Right after this, the Revenge crew cleared all decks and covered the hatches. Then the Duchess' crew did the same thing. Before the Revenge pulled out, the band came on deck again. When the boat started, the band played "Roll Out the Barrel" and all the troops on our ship joined in. It was really something. Out in the harbour they played "O Canada," and as the Revenge passed us, the sailors all lined up on deck and we gave them three cheers— which turned out to be one cheer lasting 15 minutes. The captain on the bridge of the Revenge led their crew in three cheers, and the Revenge's 1,000 crew members lifted their hats to us all together.

Before we were out of the harbour we had a muster parade, or life-belt drill, and we've had one every day since. When we left, the Duchess had the Revenge and two Canadian destroyers and some bombers for a convoy. The planes left us the first day out, and on Wednesday night the destroyers left us, so now we have only the Revenge. We don't know what course we are sailing and we zig-zag every 10 minutes. A sub can't hit us on the move unless she is waiting for us, and when we zig-zag it's pretty tough to figure out where we'll be. Talking to the crew, you wonder why we have any escort at all. One sailor told me they send the escort just to make us feel safe, and that the only real danger is off the coast of Ireland.

On our boat we have some anti-aircraft guns and a large cannon. Lookouts are posted every minute of the day and they aren't allowed to look back into the Duchess at all. These sailors have their certain area of water to look at, and one was brought up before a board of inquiry because he talked to a nurse. It was really the nurse's fault;

he was on a post that was out of bounds to all but officers, and she asked him what he was doing up there. We have quite a few nurses on board and they're a pretty good bunch, but according to the veterans, the nurses are going to have their eyes opened when they get overseas.

The weather has been lovely and the water quite calm. I have not felt sea-sick yet, and this is my third day.

We eat in the main dining room and stewards wait on us. A steward cleans our room every morning. What a war!

June 14th— A few things that I didn't tell you before:

On our way out of Halifax harbour, we passed a French aircraft carrier and were given a naval salute— that doesn't mean we were p——ed on. The bugle sounded, the men and officers lined up on the part of the boat facing us, and the officers saluted as the flag was dipped. When the carrier had passed, the bugle sounded again and the salute was over. It was impressive, especially when we cheered them and a few Frenchmen on board hollered "Vive La France!"

June 15th— The weather got dirty overnight. Today it is raining and choppy, but not rough. Hardly anybody has been sea-sick, and if the sea continues to behave, nobody will.

There is absolutely nothing to do and the change of air has tired everybody. We eat, sleep, and do little else. We are going to be lazy when we get to England; it is going to be hard to settle down to work again.

Last night on the newscast we heard that Paris had been taken. It caused quite a lot of talk, but the English crew members don't seem to think anything of it. We also heard that the Germans had reported the Duchess of Bedford sunk. A lot of the boys are worrying for fear the report will get back to Canada. Every day new rumours are reported. Some are true, but most are not.

Early last evening we sighted a schooner with no flag. Did the crew of the Revenge ever go to work! The guns were pointed at the strange boat and followed her right along until she raised her flag. I couldn't tell what flag it was, but the boat must have been harmless.

We expect to land next Wednesday or Thursday, but no one really knows except the Captain, and he won't tell.

Every night there is a sing-song out on the aft-deck, with the padre leading. There is a guitar, violin, and mouth organ combined with a set of traps, and they have moved a piano out, too, which was tricky. All the officers— army and boat— as well as the nurses, listen from the bridge, while the musicians play up on the hold. The others stand around the deck. All the old war songs and some new ones are sung. It's the only real get-together we have, but it's a good one.

June 19— Yesterday, Captain Grayson and myself were finally on duty at the emergency clinic set up on board. One of the ship's officers was our first patient. When the rest of the crew saw him in the chair, they all figured on getting some free work. We had nothing else to do, so we worked on them. They sure are wonderful people.

The war news certainly isn't encouraging. These Englishmen listen to the news, very downcast, and then make some bright remark about victory. Even when France was supposed to have given in, they were the same. So whenever I get worried I go to them and they really make me feel good.

Last night we heard Churchill speak. Everything on the boat stopped and everyone listened. They locked up the bar so all the waiters and clerks and officers and N.C.O.s could hear him.

Later, we were jittery. The crew tied folding chairs in bunches on the deck to be used as emergency rafts; this might have been just a precaution, or it might have been something else. But when we woke up this morning we saw our convoy from England, so we have no more worries; the Duchess is protected by the Revenge and six small ships.

Monday and Tuesday we took gas-mask drill; the masks are very simple things to handle, though slightly uncomfortable to wear.

June 21— At last we are here!

We docked at Liverpool early Thursday morning, and our day was filled. There were a lot of boats in the harbour and all the crews gave us a royal welcome. We were quarantined in dock; nobody was allowed off the boat without a pass. We were kept on board till about 7:30 Thursday night. When we did disembark, we marched for 3 minutes to a waiting train, with no idea of where we were going.

Things are very different over here. Nobody asks questions; they all just wish us luck and shoot their thumbs up, a gesture of hope which has apparently taken this country by storm. Tramps, workers, and brass hats use the same motion.

We were on the train all night and travelled through some lovely countryside, seeing almost no one except station attendants. We arrived at Aldershot this morning about 5:30 and marched to our barracks, which are quite nice, considering.

When we got in this morning Sergeant Poole and I were so tired we went right to sleep. We sure did sleep; we slept through the time we were given to see this place, but we have heard it is all right. It is dinnertime now and I am waiting for the parade. Some of the boys were talking to boys who had been evacuated from Dunkirk. They are very cheerful, but they must have gone through hell. Still, they are ready to do it again.

I haven't been able to find anybody I know yet, but still have hopes.

I sent a cablegram from the boat and found out later that it was a *mail* cablegram, so you may not get it very soon. They pulled one on all the boys by doing that.

Another thing. I found out at London, Ontario, that there was some mix-up in my assigned pay; it won't come through till July at the earliest and maybe later. I feel ashamed to belong to this outfit when I see such disorganization. But then, we are also lucky.

June 22— Last night we ate in the "Y," and I saw two men I knew. Their uniforms were covered with grease and dirt. They were in France and returned just a few days ago. They said there were no Canadian casualties because they were only there 10 hours.

Well, folks, I hope you are not worrying too much about me; you really don't have to. I am being well taken care of and am in excellent health. My cold has been over for several days.

There goes the dinner gong... keep your thumbs up and be cheerful; that's the way the English do it.

So long now and love,
Tom

June 27

Dear Mom and Dad,

We got to Edinburgh for our five-day leave about 4:30 Sunday a.m., after travelling from London with a trainload of B.E.F. men (that is, men from France). What a time they had! The reports you read about

Hitler's atrocities are only half of it. The other half they can't print. Most of those Germans are not men at all, but animals or worse.

We met a man from Narvik with quite a story to tell. It's no wonder Hitler has taken France, but he won't get any further.

We landed in Edinburgh so early in the morning that we could not get a bed at any of the canteens. We went to a boarding house where the price was 8'6d for bed, bath, and breakfast, but we got it from Sunday a.m. till Monday a.m. for 7'6d. That was 7'6d each, but after we got up in the room, the porter only charged us the price for one bed. That is how we were treated all over. In the canteens we were given cigarettes and had songs dedicated to us. Food was cheaper for us here than it is in Canada, but this is for soldiers only.

We saw all the sights, including Edinburgh Castle, and Monday night we went to a dance and met a Canadian going to Edinburgh College, a Canadian soldier from Timmins, and a Norwegian sailor who spoke very little English.

We left Scotland Tuesday night. The train was held up for an air raid— our first. The train stopped and all the lights went out even though we had the blinds down. There was no panic— everybody sat and listened to the planes zooming around above us. Then we started again and travelled at about 10 mph for a couple of hours.

Back in London on Wednesday, Sergeant Poole and I went out to dinner and then around to Canada House. From there we went to the Beaver Club, where we were met by girls who stuck out their hands and said "Hello, Canada." This is really a marvellous place.

We asked about lodging and they gave us the choice of several Canadian homes for soldiers. We had supper and ordered two tickets for a musical comedy called *Black Velvet* which has been playing for about nine months; we were told it was really good, so decided to be bigshots and get 10'6d seats (about $2.50). They were worth it;

we were right in the front row. One old lady in an old-fashioned sketch asked me to go up on the stage and dance the polka with her. I did, naturally. This was at the Hippodrome— one of the fashionable theatres. It was quite a thrill. Then another girl sang "Oh, Johnny, Oh" to me, and gave me two carnations.

We went on a tour through the Parliament Buildings, though the House was not in session, and this afternoon we had a shave, haircut, shower, our suits pressed, and shoes polished. I bought one pair of I.O.D.E. socks and a scarf for 2'9d (about 60¢).

Tonight we are going to a dance put on by the Beaver Club. The girls are all bigshots who volunteer for this work. The Beaver Club has such a name now that the British, New Zealanders and everybody else make it their London headquarters. The girls are cheerful and will do anything for you, with countesses and the like washing dishes and waiting on us.

The people over here are quite cheerful and ever preparing. Soon London will look like Noman's Land. There is barbed wire all over the place, and dugouts everywhere. The place changes so much each day that you can hardly recognize it.

Tell all the folks to remember the cigarettes they promised because English cigarettes are really terrible.

Love to all,
Tom

July 3
Dear Mom and Dad,
Yesterday we were moved to another camp and have set up our clinic. So far we have not had much dental work to do, but it is much better than hanging around.

Nobody seems to know what they are doing or why, maybe

because of the surprise of France giving up. The unit we are attached to is screwy and hard to get along with. We sleep right in the clinic now, or at least the two Sgts. do, so it could be worse.

Even the girls over here are no good. I haven't been out with any English girls and there aren't any I want to go out with.

We have an air raid nearly every night, but I haven't seen a plane or a bomb yet. I don't want you to worry about me in an air raid. There is a bomb-proof shelter at our front door and the people who are being killed are those foolish enough not to go into the shelters. As one Englishman told me today, "Discretion is the better part of valour."

How are things in Stratford? I haven't received any letters for a while and neither has anyone else. They tell us we won't get any for a long time, so I haven't become discouraged.

The censors are pretty strict, and can bring a letter-writer up on the carpet if they want; they might not even send some letters. When you talk to the fellows who have been in France, you understand why. It is really a bugger and that is not just idle talk. As the English say, "It's bloody awful."

When you are sending a parcel over send cigarettes, razor blades, shaving cream, writing paper, matches and stuff like that. And also put a list of the stuff in a letter so it can be checked. Do not send any money, as I won't likely get it.

I'd better go to dinner, and will write again soon.

Love to all,

Tom

July 8

Dear Mom and Dad,

I'm getting along much better. We have started to work and it is nice to get back. We live right in our clinic, with a toilet, stove, and bath with hot and cold running water. This is nice.

But there is not a thing doing in camp. All you see are brick buildings and khaki.

On Saturday, Captain Grayson and I went to Reading, which is not far from here. We booked in at a hotel— the captain could not stay at an army hostel. There we met an R.A.F. squadron leader and his wife. He was 53 and she 60, but they were lovely people. He has been in the service for 34 years and has seen action in India, Egypt, and France. Her former husband was killed in action.

Sunday they took us to Oxford where we had dinner in the famous George Inn— the most delicious dinner I've had since arriving in England. Then we went through the Colleges. Talk about old buildings— some were almost falling down, but they've been that way for years. We had supper with their son and his family— he works six days a week till eight o'clock and on Sunday till 5:00, but they don't work nearly as hard as Canadians.

How is everything at home? I hope everybody is fine and not worrying too much. Don't believe too much of the news. Very little truth gets out, and the rest is made up.

Give my love to all and keep your chins up.

Love,

Tom

July 14

Dear Mom, Dad, and family,

Your letter sure was welcome. The boys were all beginning to think the mail was never going to get through— especially Tasker, but the letter he got didn't do him much good; he felt worse after he had read it. He asked me to thank you for giving his wife that picture; she was thrilled about it.

Both Tasker and Captain Grayson would take their first chance at getting home, I think; they are always talking about it. Captain Grayson doesn't like this country or the people, and was asking the Quartermaster, jokingly of course, if he couldn't be sent home as a D.D.Q. now that there is conscription in Canada.

I don't like it much better than they do, but I might as well see the country now that I am here.

How does conscription work? What are Bob and Don going to do? We don't get much about it in the papers over here; it isn't big news with so much conscription here. Please let me know, will you?

The weather was lovely until it started raining off and on continually. The nights are cool but we are very healthy and happy. It is pouring rain out now, so I'll spend the afternoon writing letters.

Have no fear about me and keep a stiff upper lip. It sure helps.

Love to all,
Tom

July 23

Dear Mom and Dad,

I'm glad I didn't land in Iceland. The weather here is bad enough with all the dampness. I don't know how the fellows up there keep going..

There is a big inquiry going on about cigarettes not getting to the people they were sent to. Three men got seven years for stealing cigarettes from soldiers' mail and the army is after more fellows now.

The war news over here is about the same. Everybody is just waiting. Last night I had my first real air raid— although there were no bombs dropped. We were in the shelters for an hour between midnight and 1:00 a.m. What a time to pick. We sure slept when we got back to the clinic.

We went to London on Saturday, to a dance at the Maple Leaf Club. I had very little money but had the best time since landing. While there, we made a recording for broadcast later to Canada. I hope that you hear it on the radio or hear of it. If you do hear it, the man who led "Alouette" was with me. He is a French-Canadian with a real French moustache, waxed and all.

Sunday we went to tea in northwest London. The people were wonderful to us. We played badminton and I have been so stiff ever since I can hardly move. In the evening we played darts and Bagatel and ate onions and pickles. I am invited back any time I want and am to bring a friend.

There is a French officer here who escaped from France and joined the Canadian army as a private. He speaks to me in English and I speak to him in French. You'd be surprised at how the French I learned in school helps me. I am getting to be quite a bilingualist.

A Stratford fellow who lives near the Brassy has been sent home as physically unfit. I saw him the night before he left and told him to call on you when he got home.

It will soon be blackout.

Love to all,

Tom

P.S. Read the *Beacon-Herald* at the Beaver Club and saw that the Brassy

[Tom Patterson's father's factory, the Stratford Brass Company] is leading again. Hope you win the softball championship again, Bob!

August 1
Dear Mom and Dad,

Saturday afternoon the Frenchman and I left here and walked about five miles. We got pretty warm, so we decided to have a drink. We picked out a lovely big house and the Frenchman took a spell of "shellshock," which he received in France. I went to the door and asked for a glass of water for him. As usual we were invited in and found out that the lady was Lady Whitley. Some stuff, eh! We hitchhiked after that and were given half a crown for supper and invitations to teas, tennis games, etc. We did the same on Sunday and saw the country. It is such a pleasure to get away from this hole.

August 2— We are expecting a draft from Canada today. I hope I know a few of the boys and that some mail comes with them. I haven't received anything from home for a week and a half. Some of the fellows over here have received nothing for two months, even though their folks send cigarettes every week. Others have sent cables home that never arrived. I hope my mail to you is getting through better.

But getting back to Stratford. What are the Perths [the Perth Regiment] doing? They don't know how lucky they are. Any of them you see, you can give them my best and tell them to be contented where they are.

Love to all,
Tom

August 10

Dear Mom and Dad,

Received your cigarettes yesterday; were they ever welcome. Cigarettes over here are 18¢ for 10, and those are the very cheapest.

I'm tired and stiff after a lovely weekend in London with the Barleys', who are wonderful people. We played quoits and drove, and I had a meal of roast beef, real Yorkshire pudding, baked and boiled potatoes, marrow and turnips. I am afraid I made a hog of myself, eating two helpings of everything, but I couldn't resist. And Mrs. Barley said I had to eat up as there was a war on and she could not waste food. Nothing seems to bother her and she can make a joke out of anything.

Last night the Frenchman and I went to tea with a lovely couple at a place not far from our camp. They used to live in London but their business was wrecked by the war, so they moved out here. He designed the house himself, cleared the land, and made a beautiful garden. But they do not like the English people; they are more like Canadians, and would rather have an open house. They even had good, real coffee, the first I have tasted since landing.

He is too old for conscription and so is a voluntary A.R.P. warden. Everything over here is military. You can't go anywhere without seeing soldiers. And those who are too old for military service are serving as Local Defense Volunteers or A.R.P. wardens.

With the arrival of new troops we have plenty of work. A lot of them have trench mouth and some lost their dentures to the fish in the few rough days they had.

The camp has taken on a new atmosphere. Before, the men were used up with fatigue and guard duty. All day long now there are troops on route marches passing our clinic, and it looks more like an army.

Wednesday— This afternoon, one of the Sergeants gave me a letter to take to Les Tasker. As I was going up there, I passed one of the kitchens; the cook was outside so I asked if he had anything to eat. He took me in and fried me a lovely steak and gave me a cup of tea and fried eggs. I won't be able to eat supper, but it was worth it.

So so long and give my best to all my friends.

Love,
Tom

August 10
Dear Mom and Dad,

It sure was good to hear from you. Sorry to hear about Dad having to go to the hospital, but I guess he will feel a lot better now that the abscessed teeth are out.

I got a terrible scare this morning when your telegram came. I was scared of news about Dad because I only received the letter describing what was actually going on yesterday. Those last two words, "All's well," really meant a lot.

You must have read about the big battle on Friday, when 500 German planes attacked England and didn't even get over the coast. They were only attacking a convoy of ships, but they didn't wreck the whole convoy, and they lost 53 planes to our 16.

We see and hear the planes here day and night. Yesterday a German bomber passed right over us but did no damage. There is little to worry about; people have given up fretting, and even old invalid women laugh at the thought of being bombed.

This afternoon there is a big war scheme on in our camp— battle simulation— and there must be 10,000 men taking part. It is really complete, with artillery, tanks, and all that goes with it. I am going to try to see part of it.

I hope everything is still "All's well."

Love to all,
Tom

August 17
Dear Mom and Dad,
Please excuse me for not writing sooner. Time has been short and the news kind of scaring.

We have had two bombing attacks, and you can't imagine what they are like. Early Tuesday morning about 36 planes came over and bombed us although they did very little damage. I am glad that they came; they gave us an idea what a bombing raid is like.

I kept a huge piece of shrapnel as a souvenir. Last night the German planes came in large numbers. We could hear the whining scream of the dive-bombers as they came down and then a whistling sound and then a boom which shoved the lungs right in.

There was also a lot of machine-gun fire, from both our anti-aircraft and the enemy guns. Most of the enemy planes were brought down by the R.A.F. and ground defences.

In the second raid, the bombs really made a mess of things, but the casualties were very small in comparison to the damage done. None of our buildings was touched, although some not very far from us were completely demolished or burnt.

After the planes left, we went out and fought the blazing fires, but they were soon under control.

I hope I am not frightening you when I write this, but I have decided to tell the whole truth about it as you would probably hear it sooner or later anyway. This is, after all, what we came over for. The only thing I have any regret about is that when they are bombing, you have to sit in a hole like a rat and wait. You can't fight back.

To get away from this subject— a couple not far from our camp has been very good to me. I have gone up there several times, and on Sunday we are going for a drive through the countryside. They cannot go very far as they have no gas, but it will be a break.

I sometimes wish I had joined the Air Force and got some action, but I guess we will see plenty of action soon enough.

I hope that this letter has not been too depressing, but if it has I will tell you about the English people. All this does not scare them in the least, generally. Naturally, everybody is frightened when they hear the bombs dropping, but the demoralizing effect Hitler used on the other European countries does not work here. You have probably read about people doing brave but foolish things during air raids. Well, it always happens. Last night one small girl, a daughter of one of the barracks wardens, came out to the shelter with her canary and said, "To hell with Hitler, I want my canary!"

And after the raid, young kids were running around with hoses and bringing water out to the men fighting the fires. The women were joking and laughing although their houses were in ruins. They slept in the shelters all night; that was the only bit of protection they had. This morning they were around at their work as if nothing had happened.

After the raid on Tuesday morning, I was talking to an old lady who hobbles around on a cane and has plenty of money. She was visiting the people I know. She said she was glad the Germans had come; she had read so much in the papers about other places being bombed that she felt she wasn't in on it.

The more people you talk to the more stories of this kind you hear. They are absolutely foolish, but then it is the only way.

I hope this letter doesn't cause too much worry. Give my best to all.

Love,
Tom

August 22

Dear Mom and Dad,

It was good to hear from you; I have not received any mail outside of yours for quite a while...

Don't think we are starving over here. Far from it. But the food is the same, day in and day out. China is still paying for her armaments in rice and we have rice with practically every meal. You can't go into a store and buy anything special. Some coffee and condensed milk would really go over big.

While I am writing this letter I am wearing my respirator. Every Thursday morning we have to wear it for one hour to get used to it.

We have not had any more bombing raids but have had a few warnings.

Last night I went to a party with a couple of Canadian officers and the Stamps— the couple I told you about— and a few others. It was the most boring thing, and Mr. and Mrs. Stamp and I left early, went back to their house, had some toast and bacon and sat and talked.

How is the war in Canada going? As Herbert Morrison says, "Go to it!" There are billboard signs all over the countryside with those three words on them in big red letters.

I think the Germans are done for. They can't invade us, try as they might. It seems as though there is going to be a stalemate this winter and then we'll take the offensive next spring. That will be the day!

So long and love,
Tom

August 28

Dear Mom and Dad,

We have been having quite a time around here. Air raids galore but very few bombs dropped— another one on the wall for the R.A.F. But everyone is tired. Monday we had four alarms and didn't hear a bomb drop all day. Nevertheless, we had to stay in the shelters.

Would you send me some snaps? The house, family, Barney [the Patterson family's dog] rolling in the snow, Muskoka and anything else like that. Most of the boys have some.

I went to see Miss Caesar on Monday night; she certainly is a grand old lady. She lives with her sister and another old lady. She remembers Bob very well. I was at Miss Caesar's when the last of Monday's air raids came; that was the first night raid on London that lasted six hours— from 9:40 p.m. until 3:55 a.m. The camp was not troubled; the planes were coming back and forth from London. But I was caught outside; I couldn't get a bus and could have been arrested for not taking shelter. So I stayed at the Caesars' for the night. Nobody bothers about the air raids any more; nobody gets frightened. "Most inconvenient," is the way people here describe it.

Did you hear the broadcast from London when the siren went? It must have been thrilling. The Germans never hit what they are aiming at, I think because they are not allowed to land again in German-controlled territory until they have dropped their bombs. Many bombs drop in open fields, bushes, commons, etc. Maybe I shouldn't tell you this, but one bomb made a direct hit on a cinema in Portsmouth and only eight in the audience were killed. You can see what little damage the German bombs have been doing, and the raids are weaker now than they were.

August 29— The siren didn't go last night, so I slept at the clinic as usual, but the German bombers were over again. Apparently they are trying to wear down our resistance, but they aren't doing much of a job of it.

By the way, I have found a good cure for constipation. Every time the siren goes— it cleans me out. And I am not the only one. Several have had very slight cases of diarrhea since we have had raids. So I guess there is something in the old saying, "Scare the s—— out of you."

And don't believe Lord Haw-Haw; better yet, don't even listen to him. According to Haw-Haw, our camp, which is very large, "is completely off the face of the world" and "14,000 Canadians killed." Some fun, eh! I think that when they capture Haw-Haw they should turn him over to the Canadians. A lot of fellows get really frightened for fear their wives and families are listening to him and believing what he says.

Love to all,
Tom

September 4
Dear Mom and Dad,
We have been busier than the devil around here in the daytime and there are air raids at night, so we are a pretty tired bunch. The air raids are truly nuisance raids.

I was sure glad to hear you have sent me a parcel. Not that I am broke, starving, and in the gutter, or anything like it, but it sure is nice to receive food from home. Everybody has enough to eat, but nothing extra for nights etc. Most people hate inviting us out; they have nothing for us to eat. Even proper sandwiches are treasured when you get only four ounces of butter per week per person.

Last weekend a couple of fellows and myself went into London. We are all broke but there is nothing to spend money on anyway. We spent practically all day Sunday in Hyde Park. What a place, with every type, from the lowest to highest classes of people about. Even in wartime, the orators still talk. There was a monk, a socialist, an anti-fifth columnist, and a woman, none of them with anything particular to say, but people were enjoying themselves thoroughly.

We were all over London and never saw any indication of bomb damage, although there were seven raids on Saturday. We happened to be at the Beaver Club during one raid, and went to the shelters at Trafalgar Square. All over the square people were sitting, feeding the pigeons and reading papers, not bothered with the raid in the least bit, only staying close to the shelters. Ice-cream men (or tupenny bar men) were selling their bars to "keep the nerves cool and calm." Everybody takes it as a big joke, although they know how serious it is.

Going to Waterloo Station about 1:00 a.m. to catch the train we met two people who were very nice to us. When they found out we had to wait quite a time before the train left, they invited us up to their "digs" for coffee. They fed us and we found out they were on the stage and had just been married a short time. He had been to the States and Canada and knew something about us, so we didn't have to explain all about Canada. They told us to let them know when we were coming back and they would get complimentary tickets for us. The show is *Chu-Chin-Chow* and it's in one of the bigger theatres.

We finally arrived back in camp about five to eight in the morning and worked all day, so you can figure out how tired we were. There have been very few air raids this week, so we are catching up a bit.

From now on I am not going to worry about money or anything, but enjoy myself and educate myself. I think that is the only way to do it. I could go out to visit nearly every night in the week but it is too hard to get around.

So long and love,
Tom

September 17
Dear Mom and Dad,
We spent Saturday night in an air-raid shelter in Trafalgar Square listening to the barrage. The people of London are unbelievable. The only change in attitude the bombings have caused is that the people are becoming very mad. Imagine that. Sunday we were walking along the Strand when a dog fight started. We watched the planes fighting in the sky and it was the loveliest thing. All of a sudden we heard cheering and looked up to see a German bomber minus wings and tail come hurtling down. Everybody was standing in the middle of the street cheering and laughing like a bunch of halfwits; we were among them, too. A few minutes later the German plane's wings came floating down, and then the tail. People were going crazy. I think it was one of the biggest thrills I have had since coming over here. Altogether there were eight warnings in the day and a half that we were in London, and both nights a steady barrage kept up till dawn.

You may think it foolish for us to go to London— a lot of people have died there— but I wouldn't miss it for anything. These Britishers really have something!

During one show we saw, the manager came out on the stage after a warning had gone and said: "Three guesses... that bloody man is here again!" With that, the show carried on, and that's all there was to it.

The Cockney newsmen are having a time. They all have little blackboards with bright remarks on them, like "Don't talk in your sleep, there's Jerries under the bed," or "Goering collapses under weight of own medals." That is the way the whole population acts. Sunday night we slept in another shelter with a young couple we knew and about 40 other people. Some of these people had been dug out of a shelter in which several were killed earlier the same week, but you would never know it. If you have any fear, these people shame it out of you without making you too foolishly brave.

We also saw Buckingham Palace after its first hit. The Germans certainly came close, but they didn't hit any other objective they had; all the damage we could see was to corner stores and small houses etc. on the outskirts of the palace. Take it from me, they aren't trying for military objectives; the Germans are dropping bombs at random.

But the British are preparing for an invasion. Apparently, there have been attempts. Some regiments are practising getting out of bed and dressing with full pack.

Quite a few men are coming into the office now, so I'd better close.

Love,
Tom

September 18
Dear Dad,

The army post office is where the hold-up is in the mail, I guess. But you can't really judge, because of all the raids in London. Our mail goes to London first and then is sent out to the different units. Lately the railways have been disrupted, so a lot of the mail is coming by truck.

I have never regretted the day I joined up, although sometimes I have wished myself back home.

I read the *Beacon-Herald* at the Beaver Club in London, but I cannot get all of the papers. They certainly would be appreciated over here.

We received your cigarettes today and thanks; they sure do come in handy. Tasker and Captain Grayson appreciate theirs.

Lately we have been having parties at the young couple's house I told you about. I invite a few of the boys up and we sit around and listen to the radio and Mrs. Stamp takes turns dancing while Mr. Stamp passes around a few drinks. They make the best coffee I have tasted since landing here.

Love to all,
Tom

September 21
Dear Mom and Dad,

Did your parcel ever make me feel good. Before I forget I will list the things I would like best— underwear, long if you can send it, jam, marmalade, gum, socks, tobacco, *Reader's Digest*. Never mind the envelopes and writing paper; I can get plenty of that here. Anything else you think of would also be very much appreciated.

Also while I am in the "gimme" mood, I have seven days' leave due on the 20th December. A little advance in money would sure help out. If you wire a cheque it takes about two days for me to get it. There is no use going on leave here without money. Everything is expensive.

I was all dressed and ready to go to Miss Caesar's when a fellow came in with a toothache. I had to chase all over camp to find the dentist on duty and now I have to wait till he is through. Since then another has come in. I hope he is the last, or I will never get away.

September 27— Just got back. Miss Caesar invited her niece and a friend up, so we went to a dance last night, a typical army dance in one of the canteens. When I got home, there was a whole lunch waiting for me with a bottle of beer which Miss Caesar and I split. Then I went up to the "soldiers' room" as they call it. They have toothbrushes, soap, washcloths and everything. They give you a special drawer— yours for any time you come back. I also had a real hot bath, which is something. When I got to bed there was a hot water bottle in the bottom of it. This morning we had grapefruit, cornflakes, and eggs and bacon. That was really good for over here. Miss Caesar drove me back to camp.

The air raids are not so intensive, but we have had them just the same. Last night bombs fell in Surrey, which Farnham is in, and the Caesars' house shook. This doesn't bother people. The Caesars' have their windows taped, and rubberized netting stuck on them, so they feel safe, but it makes the house look something like a jail.

A couple of us were going to the Stamps' this afternoon to take some pictures, but the fog is dense and we can't go unless it clears.

So long and love to all,

Tom

September 30

Dear Mom and Dad,

I suppose you heard the King's speech a week ago. Everybody here who listened to it kept imagining their families listening to it back home. I did. I could just hear one of you calling upstairs or out in the kitchen, "the King is on the radio!" Did you hear the "All Clear" signal being given just after he started? We heard it plainly. I thought he might have a tough time after all he has been through, and especially with an air raid hitting as he started to speak, but I think he was better than usual.

Planes fly around this district 24 hours a day; they are giving London Hell. Maybe they think where we are is German-occupied territory; they hardly ever drop bombs here. We hear them all night long, but are used to them by now.

As for London— it's terrible, the places that have been wrecked and the families that have been made homeless. Some of the regiments are taking up collections for their relief.

The Germans actually tried to invade England and approximately 60,000 German soldiers were killed. A naval officer who was in the Channel at the time told us, so this was not a rumour. There appears to be no danger of invasion now, but one never knows what is happening or going to happen in this war.

The Stamps have taken a bunch of us in and made a real home for us. Yesterday they took some pictures, so as soon as I get some prints I will send them along. Their mother, who lives in London, has been staying with them for the last two weeks— she came out here to get some sleep. It seems the only safe place in England is a military camp— and she is a good sport, too. They give us lovely meals and stag parties and everything is just like a home. If any of us happens to get a bit of extra food, we take it out to help them. Hope the censor doesn't see that.

Before I forget I will give you their address— I may be moving soon and unable to see them so regularly— Mr. C. Stamp, Sleepy Hollow, Headley Down, Hants, England. I wish you would write them and tell them how much I appreciate their hospitality.

If you don't receive mail from me for some time you will know I've been moved. I have not received any mail for two weeks and it seems like two months. But one of these days I will have a run, I'm sure.

I am in with a swell group; if any of us gets a parcel, it is shared among the bunch, and money is shared in the same way. We are all broke a few days after pay day, but as long as one of us has cigarettes we are all okay.

A lot of people are now sleeping under staircases and the like, which is really uncomfortable. Imagine sleeping in the cupboard under the hall stairway with an oil lamp. That is what one of the ladies at the Caesars' does. I am going to send you a picture of the Stamps sitting outside their shelter, if I can get one. It is an old-fashioned picture; these days they are in the shelter all the time. But it was a common sight when the raids first started.

My best regards to all,
Tom

October 1

Dear Mom and Dad,

The bombing was bad at the first of the week but has faded considerably and wet weather has set in. In London, morale is practically perfect even if the people are very tired.

Do you remember Happy Campbell, from Stratford? His real

name is Bill, and he moved to Chicago in about 1923. He is now with the B.B.C. and has a troupe of "cowboys" who sing Western songs. He was in camp this week at the Garrison Theatre. Captain Grayson knew him and was talking to him.

This week there has been a hell of a lot of work. The nights are black as aces of spades and usually raining, so you cannot go very far. We might be moved to Farnham; if so, I am going to live with Miss Caesar if we are billeted out. I am going to the Stamps' again today if I can.

Glad you heard the radio broadcast. The fellow in the pictures with the moustache is Jean Baptiste Rundeau, the French Canadian who led "Alouette."

The other pictures were taken outside our quarters (beautiful, eh?). The barracks don't look bad in the pictures but they are actually very barren and dull. But we can't complain; there are lots worse.

Received Dad's papers; reading about Stratford and all the people helps out a lot.

Love to all,
Tom

October 16
Dear Mom and Dad,
I think you are right when you say I am not getting all your mail. I don't know what is wrong, but nobody ever does.

I haven't called Mrs. Putman; there have been six air raids. To go there for a weekend would be foolish; it would take a day's travel and would be hard on her daughter. They do not get much sleep in London and the worry of entertaining a Canadian on top of that would not be good. London has taken Hell; the last couple of nights the sky has been extremely clear. The people are wonderful, the way they are taking it.

You should see us making midnight snacks. We get a few slices of bread from the mess, and usually somebody has some coffee. We make toast on the fire with the bread on the end of a bayonet and have coffee, and sometimes jam and roasted chestnuts, which are at their best now; everybody is nibbling them. This really looks "war-like" in the "Old Bill" way.

I have been out to the Stamps' every night this week. I don't know what I would do if I hadn't met them. Go crazy, I think. Since Sunday we have been planning a trip to Canada after the war. They are dead set on getting there and are the kind of people who do a thing when they say they are going to.

Love to all,
Tom

October 24
Dear Mom and Dad,

I went to Winchester last weekend with Miss Caesar and two of her nieces, and really saw something of the town, which was the ancient capital of England and has the longest cathedral in the world. The guide took special interest in me being a Canadian; and when he heard Miss Caesar calling me Tom, he called me Brother Thomas. He was an unusual guide, and had me kneel on a Mohammedan prayer rug to praise Allah. Imagine it.

Windsor Castle and George V's tomb have some wonderful work done on them. To really enjoy it you need a whole afternoon in a small party. Two hundred of us went together and you know what a conducted tour is like for that number.

While we were at the castle, there was an air-raid warning and

I thought we might take shelter with the King and Queen— they were in residence— or at least see them, but no chance. A few nights before our visit the Germans bombed about 300 yards from where the King sleeps.

Yesterday I had a tooth extracted. It was an impacted wisdom tooth and not so easily pulled, but my mouth feels better and I hope by tomorrow will be healed.

The war is more diplomatic and less war-like every day; it's probably the winter lull setting in. It looks like the French are going to be rats and come in against us, I can't believe they are all that way; I think there will be a revolution as soon as our invasion starts.

The air-raid warnings are fewer and shorter, and didn't sound for more than an hour-and-a-half last night. Two weeks ago they lasted all night long. London deserves a rest.

It is about 7:30 p.m.; we can expect a warning any minute, but it shouldn't last long; it is a cloudy night. There is really no bigger danger from bombs here than there is from cars at home. Even in London the casualty lists are not as high as car deaths, in comparison.

So long and love,
Tom

October 29
Dear Mom and Dad,
Everybody is gloomy over the sinking of the Empress of Britain and the invasion of Greece. The general feeling is that it's time we did something startling. The bombing of London is terrible and the people want to strike back. I think Berlin is getting it just as badly, but I can't say anything.

Mrs. Stamp's brother, the one who did all the cutting of Victoria Regina, came up from London; he is only 24 and really smart. What he has to say about the shape of London turns me sick, but he says the people are as good-humoured as ever. It is wonderful the way they are standing up to it. Britain is more than a name.

The camp has been quiet for weeks. It seems a shame that this area packed with troops of every nationality has peaceful nights while London, with all its women, children, cripples etc. cannot have peace even during the day.

Love to all,
Tom

November 4
Dear Mom and Dad,
Bombing London isn't doing the Germans a bit of good. It is just destruction. I will go down there as soon as the raids lighten up.

Last night was the first night since the Blitzkrieg started that London did not have an air raid. The papers are as cheerful yesterday and today as I have seen them since landing.

Yesterday as usual I went up to the Stamps'. You must be thinking that they have a bunch of daughters or something the way I have been writing about them, but really, I don't know what I would do without them.

In the last war, you were either over in France fighting or in England enjoying yourself; now you are neither. We have a couple of shows but the pictures are old and you can't see them every night. You can't go far from camp; it is so expensive. I have saved four pounds for no particular reason, but it will not go any farther than four dollars would at home.

The Stamps are very well-liked for giving us a home to go to. Saturday afternoon one of the other fellows and myself went up there and helped them with some moving, then had supper and a cake the other fellow had been sent from home. The meal was nothing like the ones at home, but really good for over here. We nearly ate the whole week's meat ration, but the Stamps wouldn't have it any other way.

I heard the Maple Leaf-Rangers hockey game on the radio there yesterday, and it brought back memories. It's still like summer over here— today we worked with the window wide open, which seems odd for the 4th of November— but it wasn't hard to imagine the players on the ice at Maple Leaf Gardens.

November 6— At last the American election is over and Roosevelt is in again. What is the reaction over there? People here are glad and expect things to open up a bit. We have been "sitting and waiting" too long.

Captain Grayson says he is not going to send any Christmas presents home, which we agreed was a good idea. Everything is so expensive that to get anything decent would not leave us any money for Christmas, and you take a big chance on the presents never even arriving at home.

Love to all,
Tom

November 8
Dear Mom and Dad,
This is getting to be a steady grind, like working in a factory— maybe because we are getting used to it. But I was thinking how marvellous it really is the other night.

Every night now about 7:30 we have an air-raid warning telling us that planes are on their way to London and other places; we begin to hear the planes at about 7:45. The sky is literally filled with bombers; the sounds come from all directions. By this time, everyone who is staying in is more or less settled for the night. The blackouts are up and the camp appears like a ghost city. We can be awakened any time of the night by a bomb exploding within a mile of here, but nobody worries any more. On Wednesday night I was at the Stamps'; Mr. Stamp was head air-raid warden for the night. This meant that he was on the phone from seven until two in the morning, during which time three unexploded bombs fell within a mile of their house. They closed the road off where the bombs fell; then everybody went to bed and forgot all about it. Mrs. Stamp's brother says that the favourite greeting in the London buses these days is, "Where were you buried last night?"

Mrs. Stamp's mother and father were sitting in front of the fireplace when they heard a bomb coming and ducked for the staircase. They were not fast enough and were thrown down the stairs and all the windows in their flat were broken— even the steel frameworks. But still they won't leave London without a lot of coaxing and arguing. The only people who have evacuated London in groups are the poor people and the odd rich one who has nothing to do.

It really is a strange feeling to walk along the roadways of England and hear the irregular drone and zoom of airplanes and know that the greatest air battles of all time are going on directly over your head. And I imagine the Germans and Italians under the same conditions.

November 12— We have not had a decent air raid since Friday, although yesterday the Italians and Germans tried a mass attack on London and were badly defeated. We knew nothing about this till it was announced on the radio last night.

Friday I received Bob's parcel with maple syrup, jam, biscuits, and pictures, etc. It had been opened and resealed by the postal officials but I don't think anything had been taken. It sure was nice to receive.

The war seems stalemated. The Greeks are getting lots of action but everybody else is jockeying for position. I don't know why we don't attack instead of waiting around while Hitler makes plans with Molotov, whom he's meeting today, and Laval, plus a few more two-faced anti-Britishers.

Still, I guess Churchill knows best.

The weather here is windy and rainy and quite chilly at nights, but the Stamps picked the last bunch of roses from their garden Sunday.

Captain Grayson is going to try and get our leave for the 21st of December and if we are awfully lucky we will get 14 days. Otherwise only seven.

I intend to spend Christmas with the Stamps and then I am going up to Scotland for the New Year. You can get along with little money, but you have to depend on English families; they are very nice in entertaining soldiers, but I'd like to get out on my own where I think one learns a lot more.

About Christmas. I wonder if you could arrange to have all the family in the house between 5:00 and 7:00 p.m. and I will try and put through a phone call. I don't think it is too expensive, and it would be a real Christmas present for me to talk to you all again.

It is almost a year now since I joined the army and almost five months since I have been over here. It was probably the best year of my life; it has changed my outlook and taught me more than 10 years of school would. I often wish I were home but I have never regretted joining up and don't think I ever will.

If the war ended today, I would want to be included in the army of occupation and go to Germany by way of France. What is the general attitude toward France in Canada? The people over here have a great desire to kick every Frenchman in the a—— because they seem a bunch of traitors.

November 15— The breaks in my letters may seem abrupt, but when a patient comes in I have to drop everything.

The smashing of the Italian fleet and sinking of the convoy changed the situation considerably. It not only was a kick in the pants for the Italians but it cheered people up here, which was maybe the best result. We have been sitting back letting the Germans make the moves long enough.

I am going to London this weekend to see what damage there is and to see the people. Talk about a course in journalism or psychology or anything else; I don't think there is any place better than London to get it.

These Englishmen are screwy in their ideas, but they certainly have something. If you think Canadian men on relief are slow workers, you should see the English labourers. They are humourous, very uneducated, and lazy and backward, but they sure get where they're going.

The Londoners in the country around here have heartache to get back home. London is no longer a city; it is an institution. People talk of "Good Old London," and "the Dear Old City," as if it lives and breathes and suffers pain from every bomb that falls.

Love to all,

Tom

November 20

Dear Mom and Dad,

This week has really been a b———.

We arrived in London after one of the worst raids they've had, but you'd never know it unless you read it in the papers. Even at night there are a few people in the streets. The shows are still running, and the dances. Everything that has not been hit by a bomb, and some that have, are still open. The hotel where we stayed had had a bomb land on its roof and one at its front door, but that did not make any difference. All the facilities except the hot water were the same as usual, even at the supper dance. This all may sound very ritzy, but we were in camp for so long that we decided to really go out for the weekend.

On Sunday I visited Mr. and Mrs. Grose, the theatrical people I told you about before. They live in a very heavily bombed area in the West End, and had a high-explosive fall practically in front of their house. They are as cheerful as ever and gave me dinner and tea (at four o'clock). That Russian Princess was killed right in front of their place and they helped look after the wounded. They have seen really terrible things.

Leaving their place, I was just in time to see the "Air-raid Parade." It was really pitiful and yet wonderful. Old and young alike were heading to the shelters with slacks and sweaters on, bedclothes and knitting and food under their arms and smiles on their faces. These people don't know whether their homes will be standing in the morning or not. They don't even know if there will be a morning for them, but it's as if that thought never enters their heads.

It will take years and years to build up London again. Yet when you figure that at times there have been 500 planes over the city at once, and the buses and taxis and tubes, in fact everything, is still running, it's amazing to see how normal everything is.

No matter where you go in the city, you see evidence of German brutality. Practically everyone has had acquaintances killed and that still doesn't stop them. Everybody in London felt sorry for Coventry, which got it during the week. If all the Allies have the spirit of the Londoners, and I think they have, there is not a chance in the world of us losing the war.

We took over for one of the Captains who has gone on leave, and we had a steady parade of patients; until today, when Captain Grayson came to work with a sore back. He has gone to bed, so I have got a chance to write this letter.

I am very sorry to tell you, but the Christmas phone call cannot be made. All private calls to Canada have been suspended for the duration. And I was counting on it. But if those were all the worries people had, this would be a pleasant world.

November 21— One year ago today I joined the army, and I wonder where I will be a year from now. God alone knows, and I doubt very much if he will tell.

I have changed my mind about Christmas presents. The presents will be cheap as I can't afford anything else, but I will try and get them as nice as possible.

Talking about expensiveness, I bought some underwear in London. The only stuff they have is two pence, and for a good suit, the cost is about 30 shillings ($6.60). So I only bought the bottom half. But there is talk of *everything* being rationed to stop the hoarders from buying a lot of stuff and leaving nothing for the ordinary person.

November 23— The Captain is feeling much better today and worked all morning.

Received your parcel; you folks can't realize how much those parcels are appreciated and lift you out of the dumps.

> *Love to all,*
> *Tom*

December 1
Dear Mom and Dad,

Your £5 was like a gift from heaven; I was expecting to borrow £10 to go to Scotland.

The German bombers are changing their tactics again and are concentrating on one or two towns per night. If what the English-language broadcast last night from Germany said was true, you would have seen the glow in the sky in Canada. The whole of England was on fire, according to them.

> *Merry Christmas, Happy*
> *New Year, and love to all,*
> *Tom*

December 15
Dear Mom and Dad,

I started my leave a week ago today and went to the Stamps' with a bit of a cold which got worse, so they asked me to stay until it got better. On Friday night I got a pain right across my back and so I have been in bed and am just getting up tonight. Nothing serious— only a cold in the kidneys.

I will never be able to return the kindness which Mr. and Mrs. Stamp have shown me. I have not been able to move a finger here to help and anything I want I can have. Mrs. Stamp just brought me a cup of tea. It seems a poor way to spend a leave and yet it is nice to have the comforts of a home and be treated as "one of the family."

You are probably getting more news about the Italian defeat than we are, but everybody over here is gloating. The last official report was 26,000 prisoners taken, but it is stated that 100,000 will be the number soon. I'll bet Mussolini has a dark brown spot in his pants by this time.

Thank you for the £10. It sure helps; I never realized how much until I began living like a civilian again. This shopping business is a joke. I used my two-week ration card to help out the Stamps. Rationed items are easy to get; you are allowed a certain quantity and no more, and prices are controlled. You can buy half a pound of cheese, which is very expensive; you can't get marmalade unless you are very lucky and know the shopkeeper. You have to go without milk every tenth day and can't get anything over your regular daily supply. Lemons are never seen. And yet in the War Savings Campaign in every city, town, village and community, the amount of money being given is tremendous. It makes you smile when you think of the Y.M.C.A.'s campaign, etc. Places the size of Stratford are giving millions of dollars. In one place they have given an average of £21.10s. and 8d. per head, man, woman and child.

December 16— Still in bed, but feeling 100%, and I am going to get up this afternoon. Was up yesterday for tea and supper. It was Mr. Stamp's birthday and we had a bit of a party, as much as possible considering the times.

We are going to London and I hope to be lucky enough to get on the quiz program from the Beaver Club to Canada six days before Christmas. By the time you get this you will know whether I was lucky or not.

I hope you'll excuse this writing; it is being done in bed and is not very easy.

Love,
Tom

December 27
Dear Mom and Dad,

How did your Christmas go? I hope you enjoyed yourselves. I sent a telegram on Wednesday; hope you received it okay. As for me, I spent Christmas at the Stamps'. Mr. Stamp's mother, an old lady of 75, gave me this paper, some envelopes and a leather case for holding it. Mr. and Mrs. Stamp gave me a pair of slippers to wear around the house instead of army boots; a sort of invitation to make myself at home, don't you think? We had a turkey dinner and a lovely time, even if there is a war on.

We have moved our camp and are now in a Godforsaken hole in cold buildings. Everybody has colds and flu. Captain Grayson is sick in bed.

The bombing has been very light and things look to be settling down for a big bust-up. Submarine warfare in the Atlantic must be pretty bad.

About sending the Stamps food— I don't think that is necessary and I don't think they would want it. Nobody is starving over here, but it makes you realize how much you can do without. You could put a jar of marmalade in a parcel for me though and I would give it to them. But from the news I hear marmalade is going to be hard to get in Canada, too. Perishable foods are the ones that are hard to get or cut right off, so nothing much can be done.

It is really discouraging to see the way things are run over here. Men who have had only a name to live up to show their true character. The M.D. of this unit has been drunk for the last two weeks and the medical Sergeant has had to take all the sick parade. Too many officers have gone completely nuts since getting away from their family ties, and one or two officers who never say much do most of the work. Sitting around doing nothing is getting a lot of the fellows down. You are probably sick of hearing about the Stamps so much, but they have been so good to me; I might go crazy, too, if I did not have the Stamps' to go to.

Love to all,

Tom

— 1941 —

January 6

Dear Mom and Dad,

We got news this morning that Bardia has fallen. The opinion over here seems to be that this year will see the end of the war. I hope it is right.

On New Year's Day, Mrs. Stamp was in bed with a cold, so we had a glass of champagne at midnight and that was that. I had a touch of the flu and the champagne worked wonders in getting rid of it.

I was in bed most of New Year's Day but am feeling fine again. Captain Grayson has laryngitis so badly he can only whisper, but he is still working.

The bombing is bad again. The other night we had one about 3/4 of a mile away which shook things up considerably but did no damage. The warning comes through about seven o'clock every evening, but everybody just "carries on."

The food question is getting rather serious. As of last Friday you cannot buy any meat, not even sausages or tongue. Fowl is 75¢ a pound and fish about 60¢. The butchers near the Stamps' closed up; they had nothing to sell. I think a lot of this is caused by bungling in transport, though.

Love,
Tom

January 21

Dear Mom and Dad,

I couldn't get to London to broadcast; I was feeling rotten at that time. I have not got over my cold but am feeling better. English weather is a b——: wet, damp, and miserable. Will I ever be glad when spring and summer come. Feeling so lousy, I haven't been doing much travelling, but I have a bit of money saved and expect to have a weekend in London shortly.

I am glad to hear the people over there are not at all in sympathy with the French; when the time comes, there will be a lot of dirty work done in France— and the Canadians will have a hand in it if they get the chance.

The Italians sure are making goats, or should I say race horses, of themselves. But as you say, I don't think their hearts are in it.

As soon as I have visited London I will write an article for the *Beacon.* I will try to visit Portsmouth, Southampton, and a few other places that have really had a time of it. I don't know whether they will print it or not, but no harm in trying.

Glad to hear Bob's exams are over; I wish him all the success in the world.

Also glad to hear Don is working, but I thought he was in the army. What happened?

Sending food to the Stamps would be more or less unpatriotic, they think; it would take shipping space. I have been taking bits of ham, cakes, and tea to help them out. Most of the food I get in my parcels is food you cannot get over here and is doubly appreciated.

We are expecting a new lot of troops in this week so if you know of anybody who has just come over, let me know and I will try to look them up— if they are not stationed too far away.

I have passed my tradesman's pay test and shortly will start collecting 50¢ a day extra. Although I can't draw it all it sure will come in handy. It came through orders today that we receive trades pay, dating back to the day we left London. So that means $119, to be exact. I am going to assign it home; one of these days you will be getting a nice cheque! But I will draw it from now on; the weather is improving and I will be doing more travelling.

Miss Caesar thinks that the Canadian women have the dull jobs while the English women get the thrills and excitement. Some spirit, eh? And Hitler expects to beat this country.

There is considerable talk of another invasion and everybody is more or less hoping anxiously that it will come, because the sooner they can beat it, the sooner the war will be over. There is no thought that it will ever succeed.

Tobruk has fallen. Those Italians had great endurance in the way they ran back and gave in.

Excuse the writing; I am doing it on a box on my knees, while sitting around the fire.

Love to all,
Tom

February 3
Dear Mom and Dad,
English weather is lousy. For two months I've felt washed up without any pep or energy; I can't seem to get warm and stay miserable and tired. Please excuse me to the other people I should have written.

I was hitchhiking one day and Anthony Eden picked me up! Some style, eh, what! When I first got in the car, he said, "Don't sit on that" with a grin on his face, pointing to the black Homburg in the back seat. I always thought a lot of him and think more now. He is really a swell fellow to talk to. We talked about the Canadians being bored and he said, "They may be bored now but it won't be for very long. I think they'll be pretty busy soon. There is absolutely no doubt that 'Joe' is going to attempt an invasion."

I could have knocked myself in the pants after I got out of Anthony Eden's car. It was early in the morning; I had slept at the Stamps'. I was cold and tired and couldn't get my brain working right. When it came time to get out, I felt like staying in the car, going A.W.O.L., and driving right up to London with him.

A friend just gave me a tin of pineapple to take up to the Stamps' along with some meat I managed to get. Shh— don't ask how I got it, but I know some fellows on the ration truck pretty well! Anyway, we'll have a decent meal.

There is a rumour that we are being transferred to Scotland. I don't put much faith in it—

Love to all,
Tom

February 11
Dear Mom and Dad,

The Italians are getting the s——— kicked out of them, aren't they? People are talking about Benghazi and are quite cheerful.

The air raids are so slight I think there is something behind it; is Hitler that weak? Last night was a bright clear sky with just a few clouds to hide in— perfect for bombing. Everybody expected something to happen and nothing did.

Some people are kidding themselves that he hasn't got the planes or the pilots or that there is internal trouble, but I'm worried about what's to come.

I helped Mrs. Stamp make out her list of "non-rations" the other day. People are preparing for the invasion with the greatest of calm.

When it comes there will be a lot of butcher knives from kitchens dulled. One person keeps his sharp hatchet with him at all times. The English are for fair play but when it comes to even threatening to invade England, that is the last straw.

I bought a bottle of Fellowes Syrup yesterday to try and "build up my resistance." I hope it works; a bit of energy will come in handy.

On Sunday we heard the children from Canada and the States broadcasting and later Mr. Churchill. It made me just the wee-ist bit homesick and blue.

February 13— If you think I live up at the Stamps', you aren't far wrong! I spend my evenings there; our new camp is really dead and you know what the Frenchmen are.

Am taking a pint of milk every morning. I should be getting fat, but I have lost eight pounds.

I would not be surprised if Bob J. was in this camp. It has all the holding units. But it stretches about three miles on both sides of the road, so it is quite hard to contact individuals.

Rankins' candy got here in very bad condition. I would not send any more; they are so easily squashed. Milk chocolate is practically impossible to get here, as are chocolate bars. That Mrs. Burgess's Paste comes in very handy.

Glad to hear you enjoyed Christmas and New Year's so much. It certainly was wise to give only useful gifts. A lot of people will know there is a war on soon; if some of the people over there could only see the things the people here have had to give up.

I have often wondered what it'd be like if Stratford were placed on a war footing the way Farnham is— a city Stratford's size. There would be regiments stationed in practically all the fields between

Sebringville and Stratford, right into the city, and another regiment at Dunseith's. The Quartermaster's stores would be in Dunseith's barns and they would use the farm's wash basins, etc. Just inside the city limits would be two sets of roadblocks which would only let one car through at a time; these would be about 100 yards apart, opening on opposite sides of the road. In the ditch would be huge blocks of cement to fill in the openings. Just past the second roadblock, the road would be mined, about four rows extending from ditch to ditch. A little past this would be a dugout for a machine-gun post. Troops would be stationed in every field. At about Hunters', there would be a searchlight and "ack-ack" (anti-aircraft) battery. Any empty houses would be taken over by the military. Mrs. Griffith would be moved to her son's house and part of a regiment would take over her house. A mess would be built on the front lawn and lavatories on her side lawn. The bricky would probably have tanks and trucks hidden in all the willows.

This war is a great thing for wrecking places.

The food is a joke. The meat ration is one pound four ounces, not each but for two people— and about 1/4 of that was bone. That is for a week. A lemon is worth its weight in gold. Each person receives two ounces of butter per week, which reminds me I have not received the butter Dad sent me yet, but am waiting anxiously as it will really help out a lot.

I am listening to a radio description of the capture of Benghazi so guess I will close.

Love to all,
Tom

March 3

Dear Mom and Dad,

Sorry to hear you had the flu so bad, Mother, but hope you are well over it today.

Today the sun is shining and it is fairly warm, but Wednesday we had snow ending in rain and mist and yesterday it was cold rain all day long. What a climate this country has!

Yugoslavia has given everybody new hope; Italy might as well fold up, and the States are getting down to business.

My tradesman's pay dated back to the 1st of May last year and amounted to $182.50. I have changed my assignment to you to $35 and have sent you a remittance of $142.50. I now get $10 extra a month actual pay, so I will have a little extra to draw on. I will also be able to build up my money when I do not need it and will then send you another remittance. The $40 back pay is for my leave, which is coming very shortly.

We are moving into a new dental building which is supposed to be the best clinic in England. They might take newsreel pictures, so you'll see it if they do, with Brigadiers, Colonels and Lieutenant-Colonels galore.

Love to all,
Tom

March 10

Dear Mom and Dad,

Thanks ever so much. I brought the butter and marmalade you sent up to the Stamps' and it was thoroughly appreciated. The butter arrived in perfect condition and it was very good flavour. We don't get any butter in the mess these days, and the Stamps only get two-and-a-half ounces a week, so it is looked upon as a treasure.

I have just today got over a state of inactivity in the intestines (!) more plainly known as constipation, and I am feeling better.

I am glad the English boys like it and are being liked over there. I hate to admit it, but the Canadians have a terrible reputation over here; it is really unbelievable. I am speaking collectively; individually, a lot of them are liked very much. But we are expected to break windows and create a general brawl wherever we go, seduce all women and do anything else which is bad. The worst is that two more bunches of new recruits have just come to camp. If something doesn't straighten them out soon there will be a riot.

I expect some of the letters you sent are floating around the country yet. I don't get one a week, so they must be somewhere; they can't all be at the bottom of the sea.

Congratulations to Bob; I only hope he will go on in his military career. But for God's sake pick a decent level-headed bunch of men to be with. Some of the officers over here should have their heads read. A lot of them are worse than the privates.

Everybody was expecting an invasion of England, but that has passed away now that the Balkan situation has opened up. No one knows what to expect, but they are prepared for anything. I think fighting will be continued shortly, but where, I couldn't guess.

Love to all,

Tom

March 18

Dear Mom and Dad,

I was talking to a naval officer from Portsmouth today and I have never heard so much venom in a man's voice as was in his when he spoke of the Germans. His description of them was about the best I have heard. "Those gutless German bastards are the swine of the earth." Every word was filled with daggers. I don't think the Germans are going to be allowed to throw up their arms and cry for mercy after this war like they did after the last.

The air raids are coming regularly again, although they haven't the power they did last fall. Sunday I was in London; it's surprising, the lack of evidence of the bombings. If you spend a night in London, though, you expect the whole place to be in ruins the next morning.

The people look fresher and less exhausted this spring; it's amazing what you can get used to.

On *Canadian Newsletter* last night, I heard about the scene in Parliament when somebody from Peterborough— there goes the "All Clear," only about an hour-long raid tonight— said what a farce the conscription system was and that it was time Canada quit being ruled by Quebec. I think he deserves a medal.

After supper tonight we simulated an evacuation of the camp. In this scheme, with full marching order, we headed out to the woods and dispersed.

Jam is now rationed; if the baker has enough bread and you can stretch your butter and margarine ration, you can have a treat of bread and jam once a week; it is extravagant, having butter and jam on bread at the same time.

I am sending you a sheet of the toilet paper we are supposed to use. Please don't use it for sandpaper; keep it for a souvenir.

I think that Roosevelt is one of the greatest men in the world and if Canada had a man of his guts and intelligence instead of "we will see" King, the people of Canada could help in this war the way they want to.

Don't worry too much about me. I am in a military objective, so I am quite safe, and that is a fact. People from London and other big cities are being evacuated to military areas.

Another thing you could add in your next parcel is a box or two of cheese. It is practically impossible to get.

Will give your regards to the Stamps.

Love to all,
Tom

April 9
Dear Mom and Dad,

This is only a short letter because I am sending it air mail. The main thing I wanted to write about is Bob's wedding. I was wondering if you would take $25 of my money and either give it to him or buy something you know would be useful. Let me know what you do.

About the boxes— candies sometimes travel all right; maybe it depends what part of the ship they are on. The sausages were beautiful, the first real sausages the Stamps have tasted since the war began, and the only good ones I've had since being here. The ones we get are salvaged sawdust wrapped in thick cellophane— at least that's how they taste.

Last week we had a big scheme and were confined to barracks from Wednesday to Saturday noon. Then I got a weekend pass and went to the Stamps' where the scheme had moved by then. Mr. Stamp is in the Home Guard and was called out at 11:00 p.m. Saturday, so I went with him as his bodyguard. I walked around the country lanes with a Mill's Bomb (dummy) in my pocket and a tommy-gun (unloaded) in my hand. We were out all night but we did not contact "the enemy" till 8:00 a.m. Sunday, when we had a bit of a battle. I captured one dispatch rider. The thing was a bit of a farce, but I'm glad I went; it has given me an idea of how things would go.

Love to all,
Tom

April 15

Dear Mom and Dad,

Last week a Heinkel III was brought down near the camp. The pilot was shot through the head. Another of the crew was thrown out when the plane hit a tree; he landed in a field about 100 yards away and was still alive. Another tried to jump out or was thrown out of the plane and his parachute opened only slightly. He was dead in a pond. The rear gunner was dead in the plane: three dead out of the four. This may sound cruel, but if you think about the bombing and machine-gunning of women and children in the cities and towns, it soon takes away all feeling of sympathy. The dead men were among the murderers. They are bombing now; we can hear the boomphs of bombs and guns, but quite a way from us.

The Heinkel had acrylic resin rather than glass for a windshield. Tasker got a piece of it and made me a ring which I'll send you presently. It does not look like anything from a bomber but it really is. I am also going to send you an individual Swiss coffee percolator.

The Germans have lost 15 tanks and 100 German soldiers have been taken prisoner at Tobruk. I hope this phase is the turning point of the war. The Greeks and Yugoslavs seem to be holding their own, although they had to withdraw in a few places to consolidate their lines.

It looks like the Canadians are going to stay in England for a considerable time. There aren't even any rumours of moving. The reputation of our troops is slowly rising, too; people are getting to know us and are not forming their opinions on a few wild halfwits. Even the papers tell stories about what good fellows we are (ahum).

Mr. and Mrs. Stamp and I have decided to buy at least one sixpenny War Saving stamp a week. I was wondering if you would buy some Canadian War Saving stamps out of my assigned pay. It is as good as going in the bank, and would do more good.

This is not a grocery list, but a list of things hard to get over here; then you will not have to send things which are easy to get: condensed milk (it has now become unobtainable), Mrs. Burgess's Paste, tinned meat (bully beef), cookies, tinned butter, cake, canned fruit (pineapple, grapefruit, peaches, etc.), sugar, chocolate, tinned pudding, candy (chocolate fudge), and above all, cigarettes. This may sound a bit greedy but when you are making up parcels please just send a few things at a time. You are only allowed one tin of fruit and only registered customers of a store can get them— which means that soldiers can't get any. In our canteen we are allowed one 2'6d chocolate bar after 5:00 in the evening. Cigarettes are unobtainable three days of the week and none of the popular brands can be got. Today I could not get any in the canteen or mess so I smoked my pipe all day. There are hardly any Canadian cigarettes in camp.

A hell of a lot of planes are going over now and bombs are exploding in the distance as fast as I can count; they have been going off steadily for the last three minutes. Maybe they are guns I'm hearing, though; the sounds are quite far away and hard to distinguish. Somebody, probably Portsmouth, is getting Hell.

I went out and saw the ack-ack fire bursting, and one fire; it is really war-like— tanks rolling in every direction, soldiers hollering, and whatnot. I don't mean the soldiers are just hollering; they are shouting and moving about, which is quite unusual for this time of night. I am at the Stamps' and there are soldiers from a tank regiment across the road from us.

Mr. and Mrs. Stamp send their best, and Muriel (as I call her now) is saving news to write you.

Love to all,
Tom

April 21

Dear Mom and Dad,

It sure was good to hear from you; it's been about a month now. Thanks a million for the butter. We haven't had it in the mess for six months; instead we get a square of margarine (1" by 1"). The lack of food in the so-called "luxury" class is appalling. Chickens sell at anywhere from 80¢ to $2.20 a pound; strawberries are $2.20 (10 shillings) a pound; and even if one had the money, food is seldom there to be got. But the necessary foods are still okay.

Last Wednesday Mrs. Stamp's mother was in London during the worst raid of the war; she said she would never have believed there could be so much noise. They had to leave their flat; the bombs were going right over top of them, and one landed only 200 yards from their place. The bombing was continual from 9:30 p.m. to 5:00 a.m. Everybody is up in arms over it. Nobody except the R.A.F. is in any position to do anything, but I believe they are working overtime.

On Thursday night it was Portsmouth— not far from us— that took the brunt of the bombing, and the house shook every five minutes from 11:30 at night till 3:00 a.m. When I get home I'll be able to sleep through anything.

On Friday night they hit London with another bad raid, though not as bad as Wednesday. The casualties were high and on Wednesday a large number of Canadians were killed when a bomb hit one of the Service Clubs. One of our fellows came back in his pyjamas; he had lost his clothing in the fire. He was shellshocked, thought he was still in London, and didn't remember anything about the train he came back on.

Mrs. Stamp received your letter and I think she will probably write to you today— this week, anyway.

Love to all,

Tom

April 29

Dear Bob,

Things don't look so hot, do they? We are out of Greece and only holding our own in Africa. But now that we have all the Empire troops in Greece freed, we will start an offensive in Africa, I hope. But with the Greek affair washed up, there will probably be a renewal of the heavy raids here. It's been awfully quiet the last week or two— too quiet to last. After the last raid on London, I think the people can take anything. Bob, they do— and then carry on with normal business the next day. You might think me sentimental but you can't help being that way when you see the women and children from the heavily bombed areas; they seem proud of the fact that they have been bombed. I was talking to an English soldier on Sunday who had just received a telegram saying his family had been bombed out for the third time. His mother will never be able to walk again and his daughter was pretty badly buggered up in the previous bombings and he did not even know exactly what had happened this time. But he said his family was lucky to be living. These London Cockneys are by far the most interesting and humourous people over here, and very philosophical; what happens, happens, and that is the last of it.

How are things in Stratford? I hope everything is getting geared up to war pitch. The situation is serious and until we get more planes and tanks and materials we can't do a damn thing about it, it seems. So if by any chance you are making munitions, for God's sake, don't spare the horses.

How is everything with Trix? Give her my best and send me her picture if you can.

From what you say, the Dutchmen★ seem a good bunch. If they are sent over here, would you tell one of them to write me? It would be nice getting news from home first hand.

Bob, it's dinnertime; I'd better close and eat a bit of hash. Menu— lousy soup potatoes, and carrots, turnips, or cabbage— we have carrots four times a week; turnips and cabbage fill up the rest. The carrots are only edible half the time. We also get a piece of meat about 2" square filled with gristle and fat, plus tea and bread and margarine— great stuff, eh?

Sincerely,

Tom

[*AUTHOR'S NOTE: Stratford was the H.Q. for the entire Dutch Army for a short time.]

May 15

Dear Mom and Dad,

That story about me meeting Anthony Eden was sure dolled up by the time it got into the paper, wasn't it? He never has a chauffeur when he and his wife are alone, but I guess there's nothing to do about it now.

I really struck some luck; my 21st birthday comes during my leave, and over here your 21st birthday ranks next to your marriage; they have a big do. The Stamps want me to be at their place and are going to give as good a party as possible under the circumstances. The night before my birthday we are going to dinner with Mr. Stamp's mother in The Anchor, the very hotel Nelson slept in the night before he left for Trafalgar. Mr. Stamp's mother is quite old, and ritzy, if you know what I mean.

I'm sorry to hear that Barney is getting dopey but I guess it comes to all dogs some time. Hope the sheepdog you are getting will be as good as Barney.

I hope to receive more cigarettes soon; most of the 1,000 Dad sent were used paying back fellows I'd borrowed from when I didn't have any. I guess it's the war making everybody smoke so much.

What do you think about Hess flying to Scotland? Isn't it like a fairy tale? We don't know why he did it or anything definite, but Churchill is going to speak about it shortly.

May 16— You sure must be knitting a lot, Mom; I really don't know how you do it all. Those socks are sure welcome, and the things for the civilians are not only appreciated but needed badly.

Sorry to hear of so much sickness in the house, but by the time you receive this I hope all will be well again. I hope Don's eczema has cleared up and that Dad hasn't got it from him. Great place to get it, too, Don. Must have been uncomfortable.

We have at last moved into the new clinic— without any trumpets heralding us. It has electric sterilizers, electric drills, hot and cold running water and all the conveniences of a modern office. The only thing is that our O.C., a French Canadian, is a bit of an old woman and has a yes-man for a Sergeant; they make a good pair. But everything is running smoothly.

Love to all,
Tom

May 29
Dear Mom and Dad,
The butter you send comes through regularly but I have not received the bacon. Do not send any orders for tinned goods because the firms cannot even supply the home consumers; I did not get those you ordered before. But your parcels are really nice and have everything in them that is needed most. You can start sending canned milk again; milk and eggs are rationed now and it's going to be really tough. If

you could send some cheese, too, it would come in very handy. Oh, yes— when the marmalade gets here it is very watery. Is it the travelling that causes this or did something go wrong in the making? It tastes as good as ever; the only thing is you pretty nearly have to eat it in the bath.

You certainly are busy these days, Mom, but don't think it isn't appreciated. The opinion people have of Canadians over here is better and better every day. After this war a lot of English people will come out to Canada.

Glad to hear Barney is better; I imagined him strutting around after he had been clipped. Have you got the English sheepdog yet?

Last week one of the orderlies came around to our room and said, "There is an officer here to see you." I thought to myself, "What the Hell have I done now?" and walked out to see it was Bob J. He is looking better than I have ever seen him.

June 3— They did not take pictures of the opening of the new dental clinic. I would have liked you to see me, but the war is not over yet and there is still a chance to get "in the movies."

It is said that very shortly everything will be rationed. Mrs. Stamp wrote you a letter; I hope you got it and that it has not gone down.

I was wondering whether I could write a series of articles for the *Beacon* and call it "14 days on leave." But by the time you get this I hope to have the 14 articles written and sent to you.

June 5— Yesterday I went to the hospital to be fitted for glasses. I broke my last pair a week ago.

How about a picture of the sheepdog with Barney?

Lots of love,

Tom

June 24

Dear Mom and Dad,

The articles I was thinking of writing for the paper have turned out to be impracticable. We are not allowed to tell enough to make it interesting. One of the fellows in camp wrote for a paper; it was held up by the censors and he was hauled up on the mat. But if you think Tom Dolan wanted it enough, and he sent me a letter I could show to the authorities over here, or apply through Ottawa, it might work.

I did not go to Scotland on leave but to London. The shops and stores are emptier, and there is more damage— but it is still London and the Germans can't change the feeling Londoners have for their city. One lady who lives in a heavily bombed area told me how she "must get out of London. I can't really stand it any longer," and then, "but I really don't want to leave."

Picadilly Circus has been hit (I hope the censor won't see that). I went through the back streets, with tiny little old-fashioned shops with wares on the street and shop windows cracked or blown out, some entirely wrecked, but all "carrying on," and everybody with a smile and a joke.

The Stamps lent me a pair of bathing trunks and I have a lovely suntan. They took me to "Waggoner's Wells," an old road going under a stream where the horses have drunk for ages. It is beautiful, but not better than the Avon, I don't think. There is a wishing well there; you make a wish and then drink a cup of water.

In London again we went around the "City." This is the square mile which is London proper, and it's damaged. St. Paul's Cathedral was hit in the "fire blitz," but is still marvellous. You can't walk 100 yards from the cathedral in any direction without passing some ruins, yet there is only one small bit of damage to the cathedral. In the back streets we saw one building after another wrecked beyond repair, with huge steel girders one foot thick twisted and hanging from the heat of the fire-bombs. We went along the bomb-cratered road to the famous "Old Bailey," which has also been hit; they are carrying on in another wing of the building. We sat in on a court case. Half the lawyers and clerks were sound asleep and made no bones about it, snoring away.

The Stamps are teaching me to be quite a connoisseur of food and the way of English eating. I am learning what to drink with what food. A meal is not complete over here without some drink.

We've received word about Germany's attack on Russia; opinion was divided, but most people thought it was a good thing. There are almost as many planes going over us now as last fall— but they are all British going over to France instead of Germans coming here.

One of the biggest moments of my leave: in London I spoke to Canada from the Beaver Club. I had a lot I *wanted* to say, but I did not have a chance to say much; Gerry Wilmott had one hand on my shoulder and the other on a stop watch— not conducive to good thinking or speaking. I hope you heard it.

The bacon came, in two three-pound rolls. We had one as bacon and boiled the other as a ham. It sure was lovely.

When I gave the silk stockings to Mrs. Stamp she was thrilled and thanked me profusely. I don't know how to say this— it might make you kind of unhappy— but they were too big for her. She takes size 8 1/2, which over here means 8 1/2 inches. I don't know whether they have the same sizes as we do. She'll trade them to a dealer for artificial silk ones and will have to have two coupons with them. But if you could send smaller ones I know she would appreciate them very much.

I also received the cigarettes from Dad. You people are really swell to me and don't think I don't appreciate it.

Love to all,

Tom

July 8

Dear Mom and Dad,

I am writing this in the clinic where it is hot as H———.

Things are going a little worse than usual; we are in with several other operators. There is more throat cutting and childishness than I thought possible among a bunch of men. A couple of guys have tin soldier ideas that never work, though they look pretty on paper. But I guess "A new broom sweeps clean..."

I hope the Russians haven't disappointed us by the time you get this. What do people in Canada think? There is great agitation here for us to invade France, *now*. I think the time is ripe if we have the material. I can't understand the delay. We should have all we need and if we haven't there is something wrong. The way the R.A.F. is bombing Germany, I'm sure we could do something. A steady stream of heavy R.A.F. bombers is going over there all day and all night, every day.

On Friday I am going to London to speak on the radio, and on Monday I start as orderly Sergeant at the new clinic, which means I am on duty from 8:00 a.m. to about 10:30 p.m. every day until next Sunday. If nothing else can be said for it, I should get a lot of letters written.

July 10— Mr. Stamp's Home Guard has parades every Sunday; they do practically the same things as the army except they are only part time. They are very well equipped too. Mr. Stamp is a Captain. He had to leave his post as A.R.P. warden, so Mrs. Stamp took his place. If she is made senior warden of the district, she won't have to do so much hard work, but will handle the executive end. Of course, if anything happens, she'll do the same as everybody else. If anything happens, it doesn't matter whether you're A.R.P., Home Guard, army, or plain civilian, nor what age, sex, health or anything else you are; you just dig in and help.

Love to all,
Tom

July 17

Dear Mom and Dad,

This week I am Orderly Sergeant; what a job and what hours! Once the regular day is over, though, I sit around and do nothing. In fact, it is one of those jobs that makes you do less and less until finally you can't get yourself tied down to anything.

Yesterday afternoon I had a fatigue party of prisoners and they polished all the floors and made a general clean-up.

I have to stay on duty all this weekend and it is really going to be a b——, but there is no use grousing.

My radio appearance was to be broadcast on Sunday; we later found out it will be broadcast this coming Sunday.

I had quite a time coming home that night; I missed the train and did not have enough money to get myself a bed in London and catch the early morning train, so decided to hitchhike— about 11:30 at night. I got three short rides and then a young couple picked me up and took me to a place about 20 miles from the camp. He was an officer in the English army on leave. We arrived there about 3:00 a.m. and they asked me in for a drink.

Into their house we went, one of those cottages exactly like pictures we see of English homes— small, quaint and pretty. I mentioned to the lady that the house was lovely and she explained that her mother-in-law owned the big house on the "farm" and that this was just the gardener's cottage, used instead of opening the big house for only seven days. With my old "Snoop and Peep" instincts I decided to find out who they were; an envelope on the writing desk was addressed to Lady Cranley— some stuff!

Before leaving at 4:30 we went into the kitchen and he scrounged around until he found a couple of eggs. We had boiled eggs, bread and margarine, and tea. I arrived in camp at 6:50 in the morning— very tired but pleased.

Love to all,
Tom

August 5

Dear Mom and Dad,

Mrs. Stamp is making jam as she is able. They get two pounds of sugar extra per month per person during the jam-making season. After you get the sugar you have to get the fruit, which is a bit of a job. A late frost over here did a lot of damage and the government has taken control of a lot of fruit. (We are close to Lloyd George's farm, and is he ever an old b—— and hated around here.) Anyway, we've been able to make about 15 pounds of jam in all.

I'm sorry about Barney; I guess by now he is "pushing up daisies," although I hope not. I know exactly how you feel about it and know I would, too.

On a bus, I saw a bunch of New Zealand Air Force fellows who had just arrived in this country, and got into conversation with them, thinking they might have trained at Port Albert. They hadn't, but one R.A.F. man with them asked me if I knew Stratford. "I was only born there," I said. "Do you know William Street?" "Sure do." "You don't happen to know Keith Ingham, do you?" "Very well," says I. He lived with Keith when he was over here. So you could tell him about it.

Hitchhiking back to camp one night I met an air gunner Sergeant of the R.A.F. He was hitchhiking to London and was stuck, so I asked him into our hut and we fixed up a bed. This was about 1:30 a.m. I got the guard to wake us up at 4:00 a.m. so the fellow could walk to the nearest town for the early morning train. We exchanged addresses and he said he would try and get me up in a bomber. He had been to Bremen, all over France, and to the Scharnhorst and Grusenau. I cannot say what he told me; a few fellows have been brought up on the carpet for telling things like that.

I was feeling tired and sluggish; the doctor came around to the Stamps'. He gave me a complete examination and we talked for about an hour. He found everything okay and told me to take more outdoor exercise and more water and forget about things a bit (work, war, etc.). When I asked how much it would be, he said, "Forget it. You came a long way to fight," etc. I thought it was very decent of him and was relieved to hear nothing was wrong.

Did you hear Mr. Churchill's speech predicting an invasion by September? Everybody is now asking: who is going to do the invading, us or them?

The V Campaign is in full swing. You see the V on trucks, buses, cars, storefronts, and everywhere in public. And if it has gone as far in Europe as they say it has, then we have considerable support over there.

This place is a madhouse, with about a million guys in for

treatment and everything upside down. I had to come back tonight and pour some models but am all through now.

Love to all,

Tom

August 26

Dear Mom and Dad,

No matter how much money you have, you still cannot get certain foods; your parcels supply not only the little extras, but make the difference between a meal and a couple of pieces of bread and margarine with a tiny bit of jam. That is probably hard for you to visualize, but plenty of times the Stamps have nothing but bread and jam and a cup of tea for lunch.

I am pretty fed up. Our new O.C., the French Canadian, has proved to be no man for the job. He has no organizing powers at all and has made a muddle of things. The fellows I work with are not so hot, either: petty and childish.

But there is no use kicking; you have to make the best of it.

Mackenzie King arrived in this country, and was to attend the Canadian Army Sports Championship in Aldershot; all units were to be represented. It was a rainy day, and when we were told Mackenzie King was to be there, everybody said, "That is the best reason for not going." I think he is hated as much as Hitler by the Canadians, only in a different way. Even Grayson said he didn't want to hear him. I'll bet if Gray's mother had heard that she would have climbed right out of her grave— what do you think?

King has not made much of an impression over here. When Mr. Menzies and the various Americans were here the papers were full of it, but you hardly see anything about King. I feel ashamed every time I hear him on the radio. All the ordinary everyday people over here show more guts and more initiative than the Prime Minister of the Senior Dominion. It is a good thing he is not married; there won't be any King children.

But I better shut up or the censor might have me confined to barracks. We were just saying the other day, "Imagine talking of Hitler that way in Germany." I don't think you would have a son left if that was the case.

Army "logic and intelligence": I was supposed to get a special fitting for my respirator facepiece. Today was the day. We left at 2:30 p.m. and travelled 14 miles to find they didn't have any left. So we went another five miles, sat around for another hour, once more with no luck. Back in camp they decided to check my facepiece again. They adjusted my glasses. After half a minute's work they discovered that everything was okay. Anyway, it was an afternoon's holiday for me in the country.

Love to all,
Tom

September 12
Dear Mom and Dad,
I suppose you know all about the Canadians landing at Spitzbergen. The whole camp was talking about it and thrilled. Everybody was discussing the probability of going to Russia, Norway, or anywhere; at last, something had happened. But it soon fizzled when we heard the details, but this is only the beginning.

The Germans are opening up around Murmansk by this morning's paper, and the Russians are giving a good account of themselves. The Germans had better hurry or their whole army will be frozen— those who have not been killed.

People here are saying this is the last winter of the war. I don't know whether to believe it or not.

Today is Mrs. Stamp's birthday. We are having a drink and a little something (whatever they can get) extra to eat. Mrs. Stamp received your telegram of birthday congratulations and was really thrilled.

We are as busy as H———; everything is upside down, with more activity than I have seen since I came here.

Next week I am going to the surrounding camps to do some examinations. I don't know where all I have to go, but if it is only in this immediate area, I have seen every town and pasture and could practically draw it with my eyes closed.

Love to all,
Tom

October 27
Dear Mom and Dad,

That egg powder was like magic. We had scrambled eggs and also made a cake. The Stamps only get one egg each a month now so you will realize how valuable it is; please send more. And thanks a million.

Tasker is in the hospital; I heard it is a touch of T.B., but don't say anything. He is much better and will be sent back as soon as he can safely be moved.

Two weeks ago the Stamps and I were going out to dinner as we had nothing in the house to eat. We passed the hospital where Tasker is, so they pulled over and I went in to see him. While I was in there a Canadian staff car hit the Stamps' car in the rear, although they were half off the road and had taillights on; it was a miracle Mrs. Stamp was not killed. She had been sitting in the back and complained of the draft. Mr. Stamp told her to move to the other side and he closed the window. She no sooner got settled there than "bang," and where she had been sitting was completely wrecked. The whole car is badly messed up. Mr. Stamp took six stitches in his neck, and they both received bruises but nothing more. The tough part is they are not manufacturing cars any more, and the Stamps' car cost £285 new. By last September it had gone up to £295, for which they had it insured, but since then it has gone up to £400, so it is going to be a fight even to get a car of the same model. The court case is on Wednesday. The case will be heard higher than the ordinary magistrate's court, so I should gain a little English court experience.

How are Bob and Trix? I have not heard anything about the wedding; please write it again in case all the letters about it were lost.

And how are Phyl and Don? It must seem quite lonely for you at home— but keep the old chin up and a smile on your face. It is the only way.

The war is more and more a mystery. Although it's hard for the ordinary man to know our state of preparedness, I think we could at least make bigger and better raids on enemy territory. The bigshots say that we are not yet prepared, but they have been wrong so often that people are beginning to wonder.

There sure must be a H—— of a slaughter in France, and we should give them more support by raiding the coastline.

But enough of that.

Hope you are both well and not too blue or lonely.

Lots of love,

Tom

P.S. *October 28*— I believe what Mr. Criswell says about the French Canadians being used for politics; this is one reason why Mackenzie

King should be kicked out on his behind. According to the papers, King and the *Toronto Star* have nearly everybody against them. I think that we should have conscription in Canada, though. Every other country does, and it is really going to be a tough battle when it comes.

I don't know what you did about a wedding present for Bob, so write and let me know, will you?

November 4
Dear Mom and Dad,

I am sending this letter with Tasker, who was invalided back to Canada.

I haven't got much paper so I will get right down to business. You sure send nice parcels and seem to know the things that are most needed. But as I have hinted before, I know the Quartermaster Sergeant and Staff; the unit to which I am attached came over on the same convoy as us, and I went to them immediately we landed. Consequently, I am one of the originals, and I can always look after myself. As you know from the last war, there is plenty of graft in the army and the one who can look after himself never goes short. So I get meat, sugar, tea, etc. from the rations man. I have only been getting the sugar, and tea for a little while but the meat has been well looked after for quite a while. And do not think it is unpatriotic; it is not taking away from anybody anything that would be missed.

The thing is, you don't need to send any more bacon, sugar or tea.

I am in perfect health and feeling fit, although I do not look forward to the winter particularly.

Our outfit is a base unit and has very little except routine work to do. The units in the field are on schemes nearly all the time and are pretty much on edge and ready for anything, but it does not look as though anything much is going to happen in the immediate future.

Whether you know it or not, the French coast is being quite extensively raided by special crack units recruited from all units of Canadian and English troops. But there has been nothing on a large scale.

We see the new types of planes on their way to France and they sure look deadly. And there are plenty of them going over, too.

People are preparing for the war to go on a long time, and they are discouraged from spending money, travelling, in fact, almost everything but living. New things— which seemed necessities in private life, but have since been proved otherwise— are just not being made. This is not entirely because of shortage of materials or men, but because they don't want people spending money.

There is an enormous amount of bungling, in the army and out of it. We have a lot of pipsqueaks of officers who only joined up because they could not make a go of it in civilian life. And in the government, well, you know the red tape that tangles up in any Democracy.

For all that, I think there will be almost 100% co-operation between the States and England after the war, and Canada is going to come in as a go-between. After the war there will be such wonderful chances in Canada that it will be too good to be true, yet it will be true.

The English are becoming much more interested in Canada every day, partly because they think it will be too expensive living here after the war, and partly because of the publicity Canada has had. The States has developed from a new community into an established nation, whereas Canada is still in her infancy and has all that potential. Mackenzie King— if he were smart— could make a name for himself that would go down in history, but the damn fool can't see it.

All the great men— Churchill, John Masefield and any number of others, have been talking of closer co-operation between England and the States after the war. And I think that the two countries, along with Canada, Australia, some of South America and a few others will all unite. I know it sounds like wishful thinking, but it can be done, and we are getting closer to it every day. It would not be a league of nations like the last, but there would be a central government to which each country would send representatives elected by the people and each country would be as a province in Canada sending representatives to Ottawa. They would have control of foreign policy, currency etc. Imagine another Hitler stepping up to that.

But the main thing about it that I like, is that naturally England and the States will be the parents of the whole idea and Canada being very closely related to each will have her chance to be among the greatest nations in the world. She is trusted by both, liked by both, and so will have her chance. If she does not take it then she will remain where she is today, in spite of Mackenzie King telling us how independent she is. One thing, and the first thing that will have to be done, is to get rid of that guy. I would even excuse anyone for shooting him although I would prefer to get rid of him in the legal way.

And if Canada turns down this opportunity, then she deserves to remain where she is, a glorified colony under the protection of England and the States. But enough of this political forecasting.

November 5— I only have a few minutes to finish and have big news; but don't breathe a word of this. Captain Grayson is working his ticket back home; he had his wife telegram that she was sick and is asking to go back on compassionate grounds. Don't mention this to anyone. God only knows what will happen to me if he's sent back.

And I don't know what the H—— to think. But I'll go before he sees me writing to you.

Love,
Tom

November 7
Dear Mom and Dad,

I hope my blue mood won't depress you; almost everything is going wrong.

If you received the letter I sent by way of Tasker, you know something about Captain Grayson. It is kind of a dirty trick, but don't ever say anything. Maybe he can do his duty at home as well as he can here, but that is not the reason for his going. Excuse my wording but I have to be careful.

He is fed up with this outfit and the boys at the head of it, which is not surprising but doesn't help any. My opinion of dentists has not altered for the good. He is kind of ratting, and it is men like him who refuse to take difficulties and responsibilities as they come that cause the bungling and inefficiency in the army. Not that the army is rotten, but you know how things go.

The war situation is also discouraging; I might as well get all this off my shoulders at once.

In his speech yesterday, Stalin asked for a second front. Everybody is asking for one. We have complete control of the Channel, on the sea and in the air, yet we do nothing. There may be a good reason for it, but it would have to be awfully good. The occupied countries are in a state of rebellion against the Nazis; yet all we do to help them is send broadcasts. I think we need a shake-up and more initiative in the higher command.

The only bright spot is the peace that may be built after the war.

Mom, I have not taken off that sweater you knitted since I opened the box and pulled it over my head. And not a night goes by that I don't pray for both of you and for the end of the war.

Bob and Trix sound as though they are very happily married. She sure looks all right. The picture you sent was the first I've seen of her. I can imagine Don as the best man, and am glad to hear he made a good job of it; bet he didn't want to do it, though.

November 8— Sorry I seemed blue yesterday; getting it off my chest has done a lot of good.

Mrs. Stamp has written you three letters, Mom. The first was in answer to yours, the second a thank-you for the birthday greetings, and the third for the stockings. In your next letter to Moo (Stamp) how about giving them a standing invitation to visit us as soon as the war is over?

November 10— Dad, the cigarettes you sent looked really good after a few weeks of "Wild Woodbines" and other English ones. Thanks.

And the news is more cheerful since Saturday; three squadrons of planes flew over the camp on their return from France. The biggest raid yet was made on France and Germany. The "second front" opinion seemed to crystallize.

> *Love to all,*
> *Tom*

December 12
Dear Mom and Dad,

At last the States are getting into it! What a surprise— the great U.S.A. being attacked— who'd a' thunk it? I bet they're mad.

But it sure will be tough going for a while. The loss of the Prince of Wales and the Revenge was a blow over here. A considerable number of the crew were from the Headley area, too. The losses have not been announced yet.

I hope the Canadians who went to Hong Kong will make a name for themselves. It will do so much for the morale of the Canadians generally, let alone anything else.

We have been very busy in "military efficiency." It is amazing how many digressive ways can be found to get slowly to a point right in front of you. The longer it takes you to find something, the better the soldier you are, it seems. There is more red tape and officiousness than I ever imagined possible, and it gets worse and worse.

December 13— What is Mackenzie King going to do about conscription now? If he hedges around the bush long enough everybody will have joined up anyway. A fellow from home told me Stratford was almost empty of men. He also said he had been talking to you, Dad, and that you were looking very well. Was I ever glad to hear that.

Mrs. Stamp has not received her parcel yet. It could be because of the censors, or customs, or the Christmas rush. But she is looking forward to it so much. Do not worry about their rations; they will not be cut off. But they cannot ask for anything to be sent to them or they will be heavily fined.

Mother, I guess you get lonesome at times now that all of us have gone. But keep punching anyway. Sooner or later we will all be back for a grand reunion. What a day that will be!

Glad to hear Mrs. Grayson is okay. I hope you got my letters about Captain Grayson. But please do not say anything about it. If he ever heard about it, it would sure queer my pitch.

Love,

Tom

December 22

Dear Mom and Dad,

Mr. and Mrs. Stamp received their parcel last week. They were delighted. You should be getting a letter from them soon.

Bob and Trix sent me a cheque as a Christmas present; I telegraphed my thanks.

Rommel is so badly bent, he is almost broken, and the Russians are pushing the Hun back fast. Hong Kong is holding out and the Japs seem checked, and yesterday Hitler took over Supreme Command. Anything that happens he has to blame on himself. His generals are all gone and I don't think he has the brains to carry on a war. Besides, the worst part of the winter is ahead of him. Disease is breaking out in the Balkans and Russia and martial law has been declared in four provinces of Italy. Maybe I'll be home by next Christmas. I hope.

They are calling up almost everybody in England. Mr. Stamp is still an officer in the Home Guard, and Mrs. Stamp had to register last Monday, but I don't think she'll be called up for some time yet. Last week they called all the girls aged 20 to 21. Most of them went to the A.T.S. and quite a few into munitions. There sure is going to be a lot of adjusting to do when the war is over to get those women back to home life. They are taking over searchlight batteries and working alongside anti-aircraft batteries; they are doing everything but firing the guns. And there are a lot of women taking gunnery practice now. It sure is a great world.

Our C.O., Major Lautier, is giving us Christmas dinner tonight. He got nine pounds of ham from Canada and that is all I've heard about it so far.

Love,

Tom

December 30

Dear Mom and Dad,

At Lautier's Christmas dinner, he had nine pounds of lovely tinned ham, which we cooked, fried potatoes, bread, and butter, which we sliced and spread, a small bit of Christmas pudding, which we cooked, and two mouthfuls of beer each. We ate in the waiting room— cleared out and with tables set up— and after it was over we washed the dishes. He came in and looked at us once, and hardly cracked a smile.

The meal was especially nice for the men who eat in camp all the time, but the party effect was spoiled by all the work entailed. We were finished by 6:30 p.m. and everybody left. It was a wonderful opportunity for Lautier to be a "good fellow," but he spoiled it. In the army it is a custom for the officers to serve the men at Christmas dinner, but he would not lower himself to that. We'll live, though.

A fellow in our clinic knew some people in London who had some turkeys. To get it, I had to leave for London about 12:15 p.m. on the Saturday before Christmas; I could not get a bus, so I hitchhiked, and got a lift right into the city. I picked up the turkey and was back to the Stamps' by train at 5:30 on Christmas Eve. Not bad, eh! But that's a long way to travel with a turkey under your arm. I must have been the most envied man in London. Turkeys are a rarity over here. And when I got to Haselmere— the nearest station to the Stamps'— the turkey came loose and the head, which had been folded under the paper, kept falling out. The turkey was my Christmas present to the Stamps.

On Christmas, soldiers were not allowed to use the railways, and civilians were asked not to take the trains. Buses did not run, either, so you just had to stay placed. In the afternoon we heard the King's speech and what lead up to it, which made us all very blue.

But then we had our delicious turkey with creamed potatoes, Brussels sprouts, and gravy. Mr. Stamp opened a bottle of sloe gin which his father bought in 1905, and it was pretty good. Mrs. Stamp had been saving since last September to make a cake and mince pies; I had saved some condensed milk and made ice cream. I am getting to be a real ice-cream maker now. It was a really lovely meal and I got my first honest to goodness bellyache since arriving in England.

Friday I went back to work and discovered that our C.O. had pulled a fast one and ordered a roll call in our hut on Christmas Eve— the only roll call— including privates— on that night— and the very first roll call of Sergeants ever in this camp. The first officer he asked was too drunk to do it; then he asked the Orderly Officer to check up on us. But the O.O. refused, saying he couldn't barge into the Sergeants' hut like that, and so the whole thing fell through. But it showed up the C.O. for what he is.

Last weekend I was a fifth columnist on a small scheme with the Headley Home Guard. Mr. Stamp was in charge of our side; we were to capture the H.Q. of a Home Guard six miles away. At 9:45 Sunday morning I started off on bicycle to Liphook— the enemy H.Q.— with another man, in civvies. We got the positions and strength of the enemy and phoned them back to Sleepy Hollow, our H.Q. Then, I was standing around the hotel where the Liphook H.Q. was, and gave their C.O. false orders which I had thrown to the ground and stamped on so they'd look as though somebody had dropped them. Not knowing quite what to do, and being on the lookout for fifth columnists, they arrested me nominally on suspicion. But our scheme worked, and their main defences were taken off the road where we attacked. The "jail" I was in was the pub at The Anchor.

Our attack started at 11:45 in the morning. There were bangs and shots going off all over the place— blanks, of course— and everybody ran around with tommy-guns, rifles, shotguns, and revolvers. Very realistic.

The pub opened at twelve. Two men, "enemies," fighting near the window, said, "Hurry on and get captured. It's opening time." Hearing that from a determined-looking soldier behind a tommy-gun made everyone burst into laughter. After it was all over, the "enemy" C.O., who had put me under arrest, bought drinks for Mr. Stamp, an umpire, and myself.

I am getting to know all the Colonels, Majors, etc. around Headley, who all have a lot of letters behind their names and served in the Boer War, in India and all over the place. They call me Pat and are very friendly.

Churchill, by going to Washington, is doing as much to win the war as if he had shot Hitler. That sure was a wonderful speech he made to Congress. His speech to the Canadian Parliament is being broadcast tonight. But I don't think that the true good of his conferences will come out until long after the war.

Hardly any rumours are making their way around the camp, so it's time for something to happen.

I'm glad to know that you and Trix get along together so well. Has Bob been called up yet? That will be a tough break for them.

Mother, in your last letter you made a funny mistake. You said you were sorry to hear of the Stamps' accident and that Mr. and Mrs. Stamp hadn't been hurt more seriously. It sounded so funny, I had to read it twice; you had forgotten to put that you were glad they weren't hurt more. I read it to the Stamps and they got a laugh, too. Hope you don't mind me "checking you up."

How is the factory going, Dad? Are you on any government work? I guess it is hard to get new men, too.

Love,

Tom

P.S. There are rumours that a number of men over here are doing what Tasker did, only not honestly, as he did. I won't be with them.

— 1942 —

January 5

Dear Bob and Trix,

Did you receive my cable of thanks for your Christmas present? If not, here goes again— thanks a million.

The weather at Christmas was like a September day at home, and there was practically nothing to drink— no presents of any kind, no celebrations, "no nothing."

I hope you haven't been called up, Bob, but if you have I guess there is nothing one can do about it. The best thing is to hold the old chin up and keep punching.

I hear you and Mother get along pretty well with the washing, Trix. Mom is glad to have you; it's lonesome for her now.

We have more red tape and stupidity than real work, but one can do nothing about it. Our C.O. is an old woman of the first water. In civilian life he was a professor at McGill and treats us like school kids. I can't kick because I do get away with a fair amount; he's so damn slow you can put almost anything over on him, except when he pulls a fast one and then no one has a chance to think of anything soon enough. It sure is great fun.

How do things look in Canada for after the war? Being in a base unit, I'll be among the last to return to Canada, which is not such a pleasant thought; the good jobs will be taken.

Well, Captain Grayson has already started and I expect a holler any minute.

Love,

Tom

January 12

Dear Dad and Mom,

The war, on every front, seems to have settled down for the winter. The Japs are being held, and it looks as though reinforcements will get there soon...

Grayson is in line for a promotion and if he gets it we will likely move. I hope he doesn't, even though it may work out all right. I am frightened it will go to his head. I am well situated in this unit and know all the men; moving would mean settling in all over again, a tough job when you are a small detachment.

But I don't know why I am talking about this; no one knows what is going to happen.

So far we have had no snow and very little rain (my fingers are crossed); cold, but not dirty like it was last winter.

Quite a few fellows are sick, and I consider myself all the more lucky to be so healthy.

Love,

Tom

January 23

Dear Mom and Dad,

Sorry to hear you were sick, Dad. Hope it is all cleared up now and I expect it is. But look after yourself, especially in this weather.

I guess this price ceiling is causing quite a lot of work, but as you say, it is a good thing. According to today's paper, King is going to have a referendum on conscription. As Mitch Hepburn says, it will make Canada the laughing stock of the Allies. If King hasn't got the guts to do what is best and forget politics, he should get out.

Well, we just get well on the way out of one mess when bang, something else bigger starts. Japan certainly is screwing up the works. There is quite a bit of criticism over the Far East situation. Churchill is not losing popularity, but according to the papers he will have to make some Cabinet changes.

For a few days it was almost like a Canadian winter, but we had our first snow last week, and today at noon it started to rain and has continued to do so ever since, leaving four inches of slush all over the camp. The rain does mean that the snow will go and that will make a big difference. If there is one thing that can stop the Englishmen from their usual routine, it is snow.

These have been days of "great upheaval" in our clinic, and I am one of the central figures. Our Major, as you know, is as two-faced as they make them. Also a bit slow. A Sergeant up there is one of those trouble makers— cocky as hell until he gets into a jam, and then whimpering to everybody to get him out of it. He has been late for work several times and has been on the carpet twice before. He was told that he would have to take better care of himself or he would get into trouble, to which he said, "To hell with you guys, I'm looking after myself. Don't you worry about me." Well, this naturally put the Staff Sergeant's back up. So, Thursday morning the lazy guy did not get to work till 9:30 and had to be put "on the peg." Unluckily, I did not get there till 9:00 myself, and I should have been there at 8:30. So I was put on the peg, too. This morning we came up before the Major, and as he has no jurisdiction over us for discipline, he remanded us to the Company Commander. The Company Commander is a Lieutenant taking the place of a Major and he cannot try N.C.O.s, so he remanded us to the Colonel of the unit. At 11:00 we went down to the C.O.'s, only to find that we had been wrongly attached and that he could not try us, so he threw us back to Lautier, who knows nothing about such matters. He fussed and fidgeted all day long over it and finally found out that it was his mistake in not attaching us correctly. So he had to go to the Colonel and amend the orders. In the meantime, we are still under charge. I don't know when we will come up but it will be some time soon. I will probably be admonished, which doesn't mean anything. But the other Sergeant may get a court martial— and he is plenty worried about it.

There has been bantering back and forth all day. We have a lousy bunch of guys in the clinic and half of them are out to cut the other half's throats. The trouble is that you do not know which half any man belongs to.

To top it all for the Major, the Staff Sergeant overheard a remark a stool pigeon Sergeant made to the C.O. about him. He immediately rushed in and there was a hell of a row right in front of the Major, who was flabbergasted. The fuss isn't finished yet. The Major backed the Sergeant, who was wrong, against the Staff Sergeant. The Staff Sergeant is an easy-going guy until he gets mad, and then he blows up. Lautier has his hands full and I don't think he knows which way to turn. But it is his own fault for being petty and allowing "squealing" to go on.

I will write as soon as the case comes up and let you know how things went.

Mr. and Mrs. Stamp send their best, and they hope you are okay now, Dad.

Love,
Tom

February 2

Dear Mom and Dad,

After a lot of quibbling and playing around, the charge I was up on was washed out Saturday morning. Lautier was in a spot; he did not know what to do. Nobody else would do anything, so every day his dithering looked worse. I was automatically C.B.'d (confined to barracks) the whole time I was under charge, which meant I had been C.B.'d for nine days for being 3/4 of an hour late once. Punishment enough? On Saturday things came to a head and the whole business was forgotten.

Saturday afternoon, Mrs. Stamp and I went to see Jack Whyte not far from Headley (Mr. Stamp could not come; he had a Home Guard bigshot inspecting their defences). The buses were so darned full that they would not even stop; we had to hire a car. Eventually we got there, 3/4 of an hour late.

Moo liked Jack and the whole bunch of them; I was glad. That is the first time she has met any of my friends from Stratford. Most of the people I know here— well, you wouldn't look at them twice at home.

Moo says when you are writing to forget the Mr. and Mrs. Stamp and call them Moo and Clive. Did you receive their letters— one from Moo to Mom and one from Clive to Dad? Moo is going to send you a 200-year-old recipe for Christmas cake which was handed down from generation to generation in their family and is supposed to be really good. I told her I was sure you would like to have it.

I also told them I would get you to send over some hollyhock seeds. They have tried some and could not get them to grow; I said if ours wouldn't grow, none would.

Do you remember the Stamps' car accident? Nothing has come of it yet. They live five miles from the nearest village; not having the car is a bugger. I was wondering if you would get Fred Sanderson to see if he could do anything about it. It is now in the hands of the Canadian government.

I stayed at the Stamps' yesterday and we opened one of those boxes of honey and had some scrambled eggs made with your dried eggs. You cannot tell it from real eggs in case you haven't tried it. The whole parcel was delicious and thanks a million for it.

Keep your chins up. Look after yourself, Dad.

Lots of love,
Tom

February 10
Dear Mom and Dad,
Everybody is interested in the fate of Singapore. According to last night's news, the Jap b—— made a landing on Singapore Island but were held from coming very far inland. It seems a shame that of all the allies, Britain should have to do the retreating. People look at it from the individual battle point of view, not realizing that Britain is the only ally fighting on all fronts, besides being besieged, more or less, itself. They also forget that only a year ago this country was subjected to heavier and more intensive air raids than the European countries that went down.

I get very hot on this subject because we have an officer in the surgery next to ours who is Red and against everything British. I sometimes wonder if he is not A.E. Stewart, the Communist from Toronto. That is his name, but this fellow is a dentist.

It gets me down that I cannot answer him back, and sometimes I have to leave the room before I forget myself. Since Russia has been making such a name for herself he has been in his glory.

There is a definite trend in this country to be more friendly to

Russia but the trouble is going to be in keeping some people from going too far. After the war we will have to come into some alliance with Russia and if it is handled well it will be perfectly safe. A Secret Service man who has been in Russia says the Communist Party is becoming less erratic and more moderate every year. They have only been going for about twenty years and that is a very short time in comparison to the histories of governments.

Captain Grayson is sick in his quarters today and was yesterday, too. As a result I have had more or less a holiday; I have to be at work but there is little to do.

Tomorrow evening I am going to dinner with a man who was a very great friend of Pavlova the dancer and who still goes around with her husband, who lives in London.

It's time for our weekly gas drill; I'd better close and put on my respirator.

Love,
Tom

February 16
Dear Mom and Dad,
All that meat and fish and egg powder and the maple syrup was really lovely. How I did go for that! We have not opened the fish cakes and tinned ham yet, but had the steak and mushrooms. The food situation is not good because of the season. The stores have little to show— soap has been rationed and the clothing ration is being cut.

This has been a disheartening week. Everybody has been looking for Singapore's fall for some time, but it is still a blow that it has happened. Then on Thursday the Scharnhorst and Gneisenau got away. All Thursday afternoon planes were going over the camp. About 1:00 the first bunch came. There were 15 Hurricanes and they were streaming right over the camp, only about 500 feet up. It is a damned shame they escaped; there is a lot of dissatisfaction over here. Nobody knows the details yet, so judgement should be withheld, but our Secret Service must have fallen down not to have known about it. The ships must have taken at least 48 hours to get up steam, and yet they weren't found till they had gone right up to the Channel!

Last night Churchill did not sound nearly as convincing or cheerful as in his former speeches. I think he has had a bit of a bad time of it since returning from the States. There was a debate on a vote of non-confidence just after he came back. It seems that there is some small group trying to undermine him and they went to work when he was away and were scared of him when he came back. This is only my own idea but he was very unpopular before the war and I imagine there are people who are jealous of him now; a hell of a time to let petty jealousies rule oneself.

On this morning's newscast I heard that Canada is starting her second $600-million Victory Loan, weeks after a gift of $200-million worth of free food, which sounded good over here. But we need more men. Since the Sharn. and Gneis. incident we need more men than ever. If Hitler holds the Russians, and he is slowing them up, he will try a slap at us, since he has his navy back together.

This letter may sound screwy but there are four men standing directly behind me talking a lot of baloney and it makes it darned hard to concentrate.

Captain Grayson is drilling out six cavities, so I have a few minutes to spare.

We have a new orderly from P.E.I. who is illiterate and stupid; we have to "train" him. It is some fun, but I feel sorry for the kid.

He is only 18; his mother and father separated when he was five and he was adopted out to some farmer who treated him like one of the pigs. He practically lived on bread and molasses. Then he ran away and went back to his mother after a little while on the road. He lived with her for three months, then joined the army. He assigned $20 a month to her but has not heard from her since he came over. He asked me what to do; he did not think she should get the $20 if she did not take any interest in him. I felt like a lawyer taking his life history, and finally found a fellow from Charlottetown who knows the district the poor fellow's mother lived in. Saturday I took him down to the pay office and we changed the assignment to deferred pay.

I think this is about the first place where anyone has ever shown the slightest interest towards him. Fellows give him cigarettes and have a motherly interest. He can't read or write to any extent, but is starting to learn.

Talking about reading, I have received several bunches of *Beacons* and also your calendar and clippings, Dad. I have not had the *Beacon* with your picture in it yet, Mother. The Stamps and I have looked thoroughly through every one but have not seen it yet.

Could you send me a khaki officer's shirt? We cannot get them, and the ones I brought over are worn out. I only have one khaki tie too, so you could send one of them along with it, if you would.

Love,
Tom

March 9

Dear Mom and Dad,

None of your letters to me are censored; I didn't know that most of mine were. Boy, I'll bet the censor got an eyeful in some of them.

Tasker seems in a pretty bad way. I am really sorry for him and his family. I wrote him; I hope he got my letter. A lot of men will make the same trip he did very soon. You may have seen some of them already.

You sure are whacking out the quilts, Mom. How did the Red Cross drive come off? It was darned nice of Trix to do your washing when you had lumbago. I am anxious to meet her.

Oh, yes, the Stamps' court case. There were several witnesses: some real witnesses who lied and one who didn't even see the accident. The driver admitted going 40 mph; the next witness said it was "about 35"; the next said, "about 25"; they finally got it down to 20. Then the bench (three men and two women) asked the driver what horsepower the car was, and he answered, "85." The way they judge horsepower here is entirely different from our way, and an 85 h.p. Chev is only about 30 h.p. over here. The bench did not know this, so when he said "85 h.p." the whole courtroom gasped and looked at Mr. and Mrs. Stamp to check that they were really in one piece. Anyway, the driver who crashed into them was found guilty, and the Canadian government is going through the process of getting another car for the Stamps. There has been a bit of correspondence about it lately; maybe things are starting to move.

But the car may not be much use when it does get here. The basic petrol ration is being stopped; anyone using a car will have to carry a log-book to show that every trip is necessary. But Mr. Stamp is going into the regular army from the Home Guard, so if they get the car he will be able to use it as an army transport.

You don't know how that soup helped out, and that canned meat and egg powder. It is only due to those parcels and the bit I get here that I can visit the Stamps so much.

On leave, I spent two days in London with them. We went down the Strand to a little lane called Strand Lane where there are Roman baths in a cellar. They are the real thing and are supposed to be a sight, but they were closed for the duration, so we were unlucky. But Strand Lane is a real Victorian lane, only eight feet wide, leading down to the Thames. The road is hard slate in slabs, and the buildings are ancient, with old gas lanterns outside each doorway. You really go back to about 1850 in it.

We went out to Arpington in Kent and spent the night with Moo's mother. She has a very nice house and it is much better for her than being in London. The bombing hasn't done her much good; she seems very vague and jumpy. She has a budgerigar that talks a blue streak. One day, she had the bird with her in a train station when a German plane crashed nearby. Everybody fell flat, and during the commotion the bird kept saying, "What's going on here?"

One night we had Reg Reid up to dinner. We had a long political discussion, Dad, and ended up deciding that he and I should go back and start our own political party. What do you think? We really did have a good chat and the Stamps liked him very much.

We had a very busy day. Grayson is trying to set a record for the month, I think. I had another tooth pulled out this afternoon, a wisdom tooth that would eventually have caused the second molar to decay.

You can start sending over toilet paper again. New orders are that no newspapers are to be thrown away or dirtied, but are to be turned in to the salvage officer to be cut and redistributed as toilet tissue.

Things are really getting tough. Starting today you are liable for a £500 fine or two years imprisonment for throwing away a cigarette carton. I don't say they *will* be that drastic but they can be by law. You cannot wrap garbage in newspaper and are to use greasy or soiled paper for lighting fires. Some fun, eh?

Love,
Tom

March 19
Dear Mom and Dad,

You sound so busy, Mom, you'll need wings to get around. Look after yourself and don't overdo it.

I don't think I need any more sweaters thanks, Mom. The sailors need them much more than I do and the one I have does me fine. I still have some sleeveless ones, and every once in a while we get an issue of socks, sweater, etc. from the Red Cross.

Mrs. Stamp received your Christmas box and don't for a moment think you hurt her feelings. Food is much too valuable for that and they appreciated it more than words can tell.

I received a letter from Tasker; he sounds cheerful. Says he is going to join the Merchant Navy when he gets out! Glad to hear you have found them and are giving them a hand.

Has Bob been called up? It will be tough on Trix but we sure need men over here— especially young officers of Bob's type. There are so gall-darned many misfits that it is a disgrace, but I better not talk about that or it will get me into a temper again. I have never had such a temptation to smack anybody as I get when I see some of these officers bungling over here.

Yesterday Mrs. Stamp was sick in bed with a bad cold. She had invited Reg Reid up for tea and dinner, and yesterday morning I was supposed to phone him and put him off, but couldn't get hold of him. So Moo stayed in bed and Clive and I did the entertaining, cooking and washing up.

Reg is fed up, and he is so conscientious it affects him twice as much. He is homesick, too. We have about the most inefficient bunch of officers and N.C.O.s that you could find. It doesn't show up as much in the N.C.O.s; they take orders more than give them. One fellow you know is now acting Company Commander in the Perths. Can you imagine him having complete control over more than 100 men in an emergency? I can't.

Thanks a million for the shirts. I have just given Mrs. Stamp one of my old ones to use as a duster. It was ripped around both arms and the collar was ragged.

March 23— The Canadian papers sure are giving King a ride. I think he deserves it. I almost felt ashamed of myself when I was reading about it. The only thing that stopped me was knowing that the Canadian people did not feel that way. I heard the referendum has been cancelled; has it? And how did that committee organized to arouse the people and parliament make out?

I saw in the paper that the 1942 *Canadian Almanac* has just been issued. If it is not too big or too expensive, could you send me one? I sure would like to keep up with things over there and expand my knowledge of Canada. That may sound high-falutin', but I'd like to. In this camp we have men from every different province and it is not till you start talking to them that you realize how little you know.

Apparently in the next few weeks we are going to see the biggest battle of all time on the Russian front. Rommel is now back in Libya and Malta has just had its heaviest air raid; its 1600th.

For Trix's sake I was glad to hear Bob's call-up was cancelled, but that's a stupid way of doing things, don't you think? I shouldn't say that; I don't know the circumstances, but it seems queer that when they have to send untrained men to Hong Kong they can afford to cancel a call-up. But I am glad Bob was in it; it will be better for both Trix and the office. How is everything going to work out there, Dad? I hope it doesn't mean you're too overworked.

Well, London's War Weapons Week started Saturday— and they are going at it, aiming for £125 million, which is a *lot* of money. At the six o'clock newscast they had collected £56 million. It is really amazing where all the money comes from.

I am glad you got Mrs. Stamp's letter. She has not received your letter, but civilian mail usually takes longer than army mail; most of it is censored.

Glad to hear you are an honorary member at the mess at the Armouries, Dad. I expect you have a pretty good time and it will give you a chance for relaxation, too. It is quite an important body during these times, isn't it?

Thanks for your picture, Mother. I very nearly lost it; I was shaking the shirt out of the window to get the chocolate powder off from the broken packets, saw the picture float to the ground, and ran outside and saved it.

Love,
Tom

April 14
Dear Mom and Dad,
The news is not cheerful these days, but people take it better than they used to; the trends in people's emotions over disasters seems to change. You'd think a disaster is a disaster and would have the same effect all the time, but it doesn't, over here, anyway. When the Prince

of Wales and Revenge were sunk, there was anger and dissatisfaction at the government. Now the Dorsetshire, Hermes and a couple of other boats have been sunk, and the people are more cheerful and convinced we are going to win the war. I don't mean they're cheerful at the losses, but over the war situation in general. The factories are now 85% efficient. The country is being taxed at 60% of their annual income, and in the next budget this is going to be 70%— the limit, according to the experts. Even with that, the Warship Weeks are always more successful than anticipated, and the army is getting down to business. Last year at this time the parade square was packed with troops drilling and some had had two years of it. Now they are all taking Commando training and soon nearly every Canadian will be a Commando or have sufficient training that he can be called on at any time.

There is very little "discipline," as it was formerly known. The troops never "parade," but walk single file in small groups. Instead of saying "quick march" the command is more or less "Let's go, boys." Always, they go through the woods in preference to a road, and they go carrying anti-tank guns, which are not lightweight. They have to jump trenches, climb hills and any obstacles in their way. It makes a superman of a soldier, or else it kills him. Thirty men were killed in manoeuvres, it was announced today, when a British dive bomber bombed some troops using live ammunition. It also said live ammunition was necessary for advanced training of troops. They really mean business.

I heard today that the French coast is mined four miles out, leaving only small channels for German boats to get in, so there won't be an invasion of France yet; we can only send small raiding parties of three or four boats. If we had the strength, we could do it anyway, but to get the necessary naval strength in the Channel would so weaken the Mediterranean and Atlantic fleets that it would not be worth the chance. After all, Hitler is trying to starve us out (and not making a very good job of it) so we must keep the Atlantic lifeline open. The American fleet might get big enough to do something, but they have their hands full in the Pacific.

It was announced that Canada is building ships at the same rate as England, which was good to hear. People over here are getting a better and better opinion of Canada and Canadians, which does my heart good. The only black mark is that plebiscite, and the English know nothing of that; it has not been officially announced over here except on the Canadian radio *Newsletter*.

The plebiscite also came out on our orders today; what a deceitful piece of hypocrisy. No matter which way you vote, you vote for absolutely nothing. It's worded so that if you are not a liberal and would vote *no* to anything they put forth, which many will do, you will be voting the way they want you to. This sounds a bit complicated but you know what I mean.

If the Russians are handled correctly, they will do us no harm after the war. Of course, you never can really tell, but giving Stalin the cold shoulder at Munich was wrong of us; I don't think he has ever forgotten it. There is no use in one country trying to isolate itself against another; it can't be done. Russia exists and she is going to have a certain amount of influence; fighting will only increase it. Sir Stafford Cripps could handle Russia himself; he is accused of being a Communist, but he is not afraid to say that the Russian way of life could not work here because we haven't the Russian temperament and every country has to work out its own social reforms.

The Russians don't want another war; it would set them back too much, but if they have to fight, they will, as we are seeing. I hope I am right on this, or there is going to be a terrible mess to straighten out.

I am much more prudent and wise and careful than when I came over. I get so darned sick of these guys who go out for an evening of "fun" and get so plastered they don't know what is happening, pick up some fifth-rate tart and then tell you next day what a good time they had. An awful lot of them do just that.

I have a small garden plot at the Stamps' in which I am planting vegetables. On Saturday I hauled 50 pails of cesspool water to the garden. This part of the country is terrible for growing anything, so we just hope for the best.

Glad to hear you are getting orders for the harness industry, Dad. I guess with gas being rationed the horse really will come back. Over here one can't even get a horse; quite a few (other than workhorses) have been killed on account of the food shortage.

Mrs. Stamp has had a slight touch of flu, and on top of that, Mr. Stamp's sister took pneumonia, had a relapse, and poison set in, paralyzing her legs, arms, diaphragm and vocal cords. She was almost dead and they were considering putting her in an iron lung when she suddenly started to get better. The doctors are baffled; they say they have never had a case like it before. She is safe now and improving rapidly; her son is staying with the Stamps. He is 10 years old and a pretty good kid, but visitors mean a certain amount of trouble when one is not feeling too well. But everything is working out fine.

We made a set of teeth for an ex-secret agent last week— he says "ex," but I doubt it— and I got to know him. He is well informed, intelligent, but quiet, and speaks English, French, German, Spanish, Italian, Polish, and Russian. He has been in the pay of the British Foreign Office and the R.C.M.P. You can't get much out of him and what you can would not be advisable to write. But he certainly knows what's going on in Europe.

Planes have been going over today in large formations; almost every day now we hear them. A lot are only training, but when they come over in packs flying due south and very high, they mean no good to the Jerry. At noon today 36 went over at once. You can imagine the size of the raids we are giving the Hun now. Tomorrow's news will say, "Yesterday the R.A.F. made a daylight sweep over northern France, and considerable damage was done."

Keep healthy.

Love,
Tom

April 22
Dear Mom and Dad,

Bob being called up will be tough on all concerned. I only hope he can stay in Canada. But the thing to do is to look to the one man who caused all this trouble and go harder to get rid of him.

Things are better, and I don't know if it is the weather, which is lovely, or the war situation in general, but everyone is more contented and less fed up. The training has definitely changed and the men are being taught how to fight instead of how to shoulder a rifle. When one sees ordinary everyday human beings doing the things that the Commandos are doing it is unbelievable. They belong to the pioneer days when a farmer had to walk a couple of hundred miles to do his shopping. Some of the regiments in the field are now on a 200-mile route march.

The Commandos of this camp are just taking the preliminary course. Even at that live ammunition is used and when the order "take cover" comes, that is what it means— or else! Last Saturday a village in this neighbourhood was raided and everybody cleared out. The civilians were not forewarned and some of them thought the invasion had really come.

At the clinic we have two new operators, so there is less work to do. We were rushed for a while and really earned our money, but things are back to normal.

Last weekend we received the draft from which the 400 men left the boat at Halifax. They said something went wrong with the rations and they did not have any food for 24 hours, but I don't know how true that is.

Mrs. Stamp is being interviewed at the Labour Exchange this afternoon. I think she will only have to do part-time work; she has a husband living at home. She is in "Group 2," known as "Immobile Women." Quite a title, eh? I hope she does not have to do any heavy work; it would ruin her. She is healthy enough, but not exceedingly strong.

The whole country is going more "austere," as the papers say. Another cut in the meat ration has been announced; pretty soon it won't be worth going to the store at all. But we are being fed much better than one might think, and much much better than anyone else in Europe.

Taking everything into consideration, I think our chances for a quick victory are good. I hope I am right. Everyone seems to be thinking that these days and yet they are more willing to work for it. I don't think any country in the world has ever put such wholehearted, good natured work into any war, nor have they given up so much without kicking. And they are anxious to give up still more if it will help.

Mr. Stamp's sister is on the road to recovery and has become something of a "guinea pig" to the medical students at the hospital.

No one seems to know what she had or why. We had some of the lemon and other fruit juice you sent. Mr. Stamp's mother tried all over London to get some but could not.

I don't know how you find all the nice things you put in the parcels, but they sure are good and are more than appreciated. Last night we had some pancakes with maple syrup and on the weekend are going to make a raisin pie with the raisins you sent.

Mother, I will be able to take over your job as cook when I go home. I am becoming good at it. When the cupboard at the Stamps' gets rather bare and Mrs. Stamp runs out of ideas, I go to town and with her help, manage to make something. Ice cream is my specialty, but I make pancakes, steamed puddings, hamburgers, buns and cakes. All your boxes help, and I could not do anything without them.

Here is my recipe for hamburgers: one tin bully beef, onion flavouring and onion salt, Worcestershire sauce and any other kind of spice you can lay your hands on, herbs, egg powder and milk, boiled and slightly creamed potatoes, salt and pepper. I throw it all in a bowl and mix thoroughly, roll into patties, cover with flour and fry.

They really are delicious.

But I have just been notified that I am to go down and vote to see whether I can make MacKenzie King a good fellow or a liar.

Love,
Tom

April 28
Dear Mom and Dad,
We are bombing more and more of Germany and France and last weekend the Germans blitzed Bath in a "reprisal" raid. Their raids are nothing now compared to last year's; they haven't got the same

number of planes. There is a lot of agitation for a second front in Europe from quite high circles. Lord Beaverbrook's speech in New York was received enthusiastically and all the English papers are quoting him.

The way they are training the troops indicates that the "second front" may be started soon. The countries under Germany are giving more trouble and even Germany seems to be cracking a bit. On Sunday Hitler made an unexpected speech in which he set himself up as God Almighty.

Soon only utility clothes will be sold here. They are nothing to go crazy over but are not too bad. Everybody is taking it cheerfully, realizing the extent they must sacrifice— that is, almost everything— if they want to win this war quickly.

But to get away from the war— the sun has been shining steadily. Everyone is talking about the "dry spell" and hoping it will rain soon, but it looks a good season for the crops. Even my radishes and lettuce are coming up. I have a few more things to plant and hope to get it done this week.

Captain Grayson is running the unit ball team again this year and is taking time off for coaching, which is how I had time to start this letter this morning.

Tomorrow I get two inoculations and then the afternoon off. I expect I will be feeling pretty tough; we get two different kinds at once. But outside of that I am as healthy as can be.

Next weekend we are all going to be C.B.'d for a scheme. I think it is the same as the one last summer only bigger and more realistic. I don't think any live ammunition will be used here; this is a base camp and our job will be receiving "casualties" and dispatching "reinforcements."

This thing would come when I was going out to a meal with the Stamps.

Mr. Stamp's sister is practically well now and Sunday she phoned the Stamps. I was talking to her and she thanked me very much for the fruit juice. She said an American doctor was working in the hospital, and when he saw the tin of lemon juice, he nearly went mad with jealousy. It is a miracle how she ever pulled through, but she is recuperating quickly, and her son went home yesterday.

How are Bob and Trix getting along? I hope they can be together and not too far from Stratford. Are Don and Phyl home very often? I hope they are. It must be lonely for you with nobody about. But cheer up and hope for the best.

Love,

Tom

May 4

Dear Mom and Dad,

I guess you are both missing Bob and Trix quite a bit. It sure is a shame but the longer this b——— war goes on the more one has to make up one's mind to put up with it and work harder for the finish.

Just after I joined up Mary Harrison told me what a fool I was for rushing into it. I told her that there would be a lot of fellows hanging back then who would have to take ordinary privates' jobs when they did have to join, but she would not believe me.

My job isn't anything much but it is still better than a lot of officers' jobs, and they will have to start fresh after the war whereas I can carry on at what I am doing. A new educational course has just started over here and I am going to apply for one in dentistry. It doesn't give you a degree or anything like that, but prepares one for university. From what I hear they will give us a year at university free and then graduate us, which sounds too good to be true, and there will be many who will not deserve their degree, but it is worth working on.

What do you think of the result of the plebiscite? I guess the vote was no surprise to anyone; it should never have been held.

There was a rumour around the camp that all the letters were being censored, but I guess it fell through, if there was anything in it. I heard of one case where a soldier sent home for $20 worth of cigarettes, saying he could get $100 for them over here. They stopped the letter and court martialled him.

Due to good weather the planes have been going over steadily for days. There are some going over right now, so high up that only a low drum–drum can be heard. Every day and all night the fighters can be seen, often not 1,000 feet up.

Love,
Tom

May 18
Dear Mom and Dad,
It is a good thing that Bob and Trix can be together. I hope they can stay that way for the duration.

I told Mrs. Stamp you had not heard from her and she was very disappointed; she has written three times since Christmas. By the way, Moo's birthday is September 12. Thought I better tell you before I forgot.

Captain Grayson was telling me that his wife asked if he had met the Stamps yet. He has met them once and that was not my fault. I do not want to take him there any more than he wants to go. You see there is no "gay life" there, and that is all that interests him. Don't let that out, but he is living up to his reputation.

Last week I arranged for my course in dentistry. It is not really dentistry yet, but the subjects I will take are those needed before the full course can be completed. I will not be able to take any of the technical courses yet, but I can get off time for those when I get back.

Yesterday the troops over here started on their first offensive scheme. Up till now, everything has been planned on the idea of repelling the invader. This time it is the exact opposite. All the troops from this camp with the exception of the H.Q. staff have left and expect to be away three weeks. In the meantime we can take it comparatively easy. But Colonel Lott is expected here this week, so we have to be on our toes. He is an Ottawa bigshot— not only in the army but in the dental profession. Everybody is a-dither trying to make a good impression. There are going to be drastic changes in the set-up of our unit, and all the officers are watching closely to see if they can't get promotions etc. Lott sounds a very business-like man. Lautier, our C.O., doesn't know which way to turn. He has been checked on so many things now that he is frightened to think about doing anything. But he may go back to Canada soon and we won't have to worry about him. Then the big thing will be, "who will get his job?" Grayson is in the running, but it would not surprise me if he did not get it. The air will be blue if that happens.

I thought, with the camp about empty, we would have a fairly easy time, but no matter what happens, some men can always be raked in. Grayson does not want me writing letters during duty hours— even when there is nothing to do— in case Lott comes in.

Am enclosing some $1 stamps for Grandma. I remembered!

Love,

Tom

May 25

Dear Mom and Dad,

Your parcel was lovely, and a real "contribution to the cause." You don't know how much they are looked forward to. That noodle soup was the saviour of an otherwise empty meal. Everything along that line is harder and harder to get. Your idea of a "basic" parcel should be adopted by everyone: butter, eggs, tinned milk, noodle soup, candy, and occasional extras, like sandwich spread (very useful in an emergency as we can get lots of bread), tinned onions, meat; this is just about as much as anyone could ask for. The book made your parcel that much better.

We are geared right up to war pitch; if the shirkers you speak of over there were brought over here for a week, they'd soon learn what war means. The last week or so I have been comparing the differences between war and peace as applied to the ordinary civilian— if you could call anyone that now!— and it is really marvellous the way the English people are living their daily lives. Even the bus service has been cut down, travelling of any kind is discouraged, all non-essential cars will be off the road next month, and non-essential means exactly that. One man is a foreman in a construction company building military camps etc.; his home is seven miles from his office and from there he has to visit the different projects. To use a car he has to get a special license and is allowed only six gallons of petrol a month. Figure it out. And there will be no increase in the bus service when the cars are taken off the road.

Every food that is not directly rationed is on a points system, and each person is allowed 24 points a month. A tin of pears or plums is 16 points. To get rice, meat loaf, bully beef, canned salmon, cereals and almost everything else, you have to surrender points. There is not much to eat in the way of extras. This shows also how much your parcels are appreciated.

But people are more aggressive and more anxious to start a second front than they have ever been before. Sometimes I get so fed up with living an almost "civilian in khaki" life that I would like to swim the Channel and shoot a few Germans myself. But as one of the papers over here says, "the Canadians have one of the hardest jobs of the war just sitting and guarding, and are making a swell job of it."

I guess the new conscription bill will wake a few people up over there. And I guess you will hear a lot of resentment about "Why they called my boy up." But let me tell you a story of an ordinary middle-class woman living near the Stamps'. She is married and had one son. Her son went into the R.A.F. as a pilot. Shortly after this, the woman's sister was evacuated from London and sent to her; the sister was very ill and needed nursing. Then the woman's husband went to the hospital for a very serious operation; days after that her only son was killed. Her husband returned from the hospital three months ago, after months in bed. The woman's sister died. The husband still has to go to the doctor daily to have the dressings changed. (His operation was on a war wound.) And she still always speaks with a smile. She has said that if she had five more sons she would gladly give them.

Two ladies over 70 live across from the Stamps'. They spent most of their lives in the tea-planting business in Burma. All their money was tied up there and their brother was running the business. Now they have not got a penny and know nothing of their brother. So the one old lady is staying to look after the house while the other is out looking for a job. She applied for one of helper at a dentist's, but was turned down. She is collecting silver paper etc. as salvage and is getting program information from the public for the B.B.C. (a sort of polling). If that isn't a fine example of British spirit, I don't know what could be. And those are not isolated cases. Every second house in Headley has some kind of trouble and there is hardly one of them crying about it. But enough of that.

I have not heard from Bob, but I'm writing him tonight. I hope he and Trix can be together after he leaves B.C.

I had no idea the *Canadian Almanac* cost so much and I am sorry I asked for it lightly. I thought it was like one of those little books Dad used to get— "Facts About Canada" or something like that.

The weather here has been God-awful, blowing like H—— and raining hard.

Love,
Tom

June 1
Dear Mom and Dad,

A good thing— any Perths will come to this camp. If Bob gets over here we will be very close together, for a short time, anyway. But I'm sorry Bob ever had to join up.

Grayson does not like the idea of the Perths coming so near because, as he says, he has to look out for himself. He told me not to say anything, but it won't make any difference; everybody knows how he has been acting. As long as he keeps kidding himself, I guess he will be happy.

How is the anti-British feeling in the States? I should think it is among the loud-mouthed minority, but some people say it is very widespread.

What do you think of the raid on Cologne on Saturday night? I hope by the time you get this, you will be saying which one, but this was the first raid of over 1,000 planes. It sure must have been hot around there for a while and everyone seems very pleased with it. It seems bad to be pleased with such destruction, but the more of those raids we can have, the sooner the war will be over, and that should be everybody's ultimate aim. I have just finished reading *The Failure of a Mission*, a book by Sir Neville Henderson, the British Ambassador to Germany. It is really good and gives a good insight into the German character and the causes of the war.

About the dentistry course I'll be taking when I get home: besides all medical and dental care for a year, we get a clothing allowance, rehabilitation grant, our fees paid and Unemployment Insurance of $9 a week to live on. With the money I have saved I should do all right. The future looks good if it can only last.

You seem to be very busy, Dad. I guess war work means an awful lot of red tape. Take care of yourself and don't overdo it.

By the end of this week we should be getting radishes, onions, lettuce, and beets from my garden at the Stamps'. You will be very busy with your garden by now, too, Mom. I hope you aren't going at it too strenuously.

I have not heard from Tasker for quite a while. Is he in a very bad way?

How is the Quebec–Canada war coming along? I hope the conscription bill gets through with the least amount of friction being caused.

Right now I am smoking borrowed cigarettes and hope some come through before I run out.

The Stamps send their best...

Love,
Tom

June 11

Dear Mom and Dad,

I seemed to have a sort of "sleeping sickness" earlier this week; I could hardly keep my eyes open, so went to bed early. Anyway, about six last night, word came that our Staff Sergeant was to pack up and leave by 10:00 this morning. The Staff happened to be out and did not get in till about 11:30, which meant some fast work. This morning, as usual, his departure was postponed till 2:00, and then till 10:00 a.m. tomorrow. But that is the army.

Then, at 11:00 this morning, we heard that Colonel Lott, the Director of Dental Services, was coming here this afternoon. We spent the whole noon hour cleaning. He *did* get here, and what a bombshell he dropped! Major Lautier got his walking— or should I say boating— ticket, and guess what? Captain C. H. Grayson is to be the new C.O. I am glad to see Lautier go but am afraid Grayson will lose his head still more; on the other hand, he may accept the responsibility and settle down. I shouldn't look only to the bad side of things. There is a very slight chance that I may be promoted myself, but it is very slight; chair assistants are more or less frowned upon as far as promotion goes.

My birthday parcel was about the best yet. The macaroni and cheese was a delicious meal in itself. The niblets were something you dream of. The corn seed, I hope, I will be able to tell you all about at the end of the summer. Moo got her stockings and Clive his tobacco, and both were more than pleased.

Mother, don't ever worry about me being a fatalist. In fact, I think your worries should go to the other end. Most of the time I paint the picture too rosily, but I always say that if you aim for the stars and only get halfway there you are still heads above. I am counting on returning to Canada and being a good Canadian citizen, if not more. There I go, shooting for the stars again.

I would appreciate those books on Canada's war effort, and I never got the *Beacon* with Bob's write-up in it. A lot of stuff was destroyed through enemy action, so I guess the whales are reading about Bob now.

Love,

Tom

P.S. It was just two years ago that I sailed from Halifax and two years and one week since I left home. It sure seems a long time, but I hope that I can be back before the next anniversary.

June 30

Dear Mom and Dad,

Well, the bantam corn has started. There are now 17 shoots up and it looks very healthy. My garden has been fairly successful up till now. We have had radishes and a few very small onions. Last Saturday I transplanted some lettuce and it is doing fine. The beets are coming along, but they're not ready yet. The weather has been beautiful, but you can never count on English weather; if June is a good month, it is a fair indication that July and August will not be. But that is looking on the black side of things, isn't it?

I have just put on my respirator. Everybody has to wear it from 10:00 to 10:30 Tuesday mornings. As you can imagine, it is not too comfortable.

It certainly is good to hear of these 1,000-plane raids, isn't it? I hope they can keep it up continually as they will do 100% more to hurt German morale than spasmodic raids.

When I told you not to send any more lemon, I meant lemon barley and tinned dried lemon; but the canned lemon juice does not take as much sugar; in fact, we discovered a new way to mix it which does not take any sugar.

The increase in babies is not confined to Canada. There are as many illegitimate children being born over here as there are Germans being killed in Russia. That is an exaggeration, but people here don't mind in the least; a mother may be a bit annoyed with her daughter, and that is all.

About the war: if it hadn't been for those countries sitting on the fence hoping for the best, the war might have been over by now. But I guess we are all to blame, so the only thing is to see that the same thing doesn't happen again.

According to the papers you are facing the pinch of war in the food line now. It is too bad and yet it will probably do a lot of good to those people who sit around and think this is somebody else's war. Bacon is sure expensive at 54¢, isn't it? Doesn't it come under price control? I told that to Mrs. Stamp and she said that was the ordinary price in peacetime over here. Really, the Canadian people don't know how lucky they are. Your main trouble will be tea, won't it? Especially you, Mother.

The big change in our establishment has taken place. We are now a company, and Captain Gray is in charge of this clinic. The changeover has made little difference to me, except that soon I may have an entirely new job on the administrative end. But I'll have to wait and see.

I've had seven days leave that I enjoyed more than any other leave over here. I bought a bike and while Clive was away Moo and I bicycled around the country lanes. I now know what the poet meant when he said, "Oh, to be in England now that June is here." It was a joy to feel like a civilian again, away from all the khaki. Most of the time we had no idea where we were going, but would make up our minds to take "the first road on the left" and see where we ended up. And in that way we really saw the country. The English gardens are in full bloom and there are millions of roses of all kinds.

Moo had not ridden a bike since she was fourteen and her seat was sore. But Sunday we went out to the ranges where Clive was giving bombing instruction to a group of Home Guard; at noon we had a drink in the pub and then a lovely old-fashioned picnic at the edge of the range, with that lovely hay smell everywhere.

So now back to work for another three months.

I've tasted that vegetable juice you sent and it is delicious. You sure do know how to make up the parcels; every one has surprises in it. Thanks a million.

The corn is coming along wonderfully. I counted the shoots last night and there were 29 in the first bunch I planted. The second lot should be coming along any day now as they were put in about five days later. I hope they were planted in time to produce corn. In case they are late, could you send me the recipe for pickling young cobs, Mother?

Once again, the war situation seems worse, but it is still remarkable that we are where we are. When I first came over there was not an anti-aircraft gun to be seen anywhere, and in yesterday's debate in Parliament it was disclosed that we had had no tanks, very few big guns, and only five fighter planes in reserve; more than that, we had no allies. During the Battle of Britain, which lasted six months, everything was in disorder, and the people were tired and worn out, although they did not admit it. A year and a half later, we are talking about a second front and waging war in every corner of the world.

Love,

Tom

July 7

Dear Mom and Dad,

You mentioned in your letter that you thought I liked strawberry jam. I love it, especially yours; it is so much like real strawberries. But how do you manage the sugar? Last week Mrs. Stamp made gooseberry jam and it turned out well, but there was not very much. She has also bottled some fruit. This year fruit is more plentiful than it has been.

My garden is coming along; if the corn keeps on this way, I'll have to think about stopping it before it gets too high to take off the cobs. Last week there were 28 shoots; last night I counted 196.

On Sunday I visited Mr. Stamp's sister (the one who was so sick); she has lost a lot of weight, of course, but looks quite happy and healthy. She told me to thank you again for the fruit juice and for your good wishes, which I gave her.

The sky over here is thudding with planes on their way to France or Germany. That noise does one's heart good these days.

About B.C., though, I hear the Canadian G.H.Q. has been moved from Vancouver Island to the mainland. Do you think they are preparing for an invasion? I hope not. The only good thing about that would be the "awakening of King." Or do you think they'd have to attack Ottawa to bring him out of his daze?

It must be quite a pleasant change, Dad, to have customers running to you for orders, especially after the last few years. I hope you can do all right out of it.

Well, I have a new job, temporarily. I am now Acting Staff Sergeant, Quartermaster Sergeant, and clerk. Great combination, don't you think? It's not as bad as it sounds. I have an office to myself and look after stores for the clinic. It is good experience; one gets to know the inside of the business, which will do me good if I practise dentistry.

Love,

Tom

July 16
Dear Mom and Dad,

Bet this will be a surprise for you, but it is really me. As you see, I have become quite the typer.

About my course in dentistry, I have heard nothing more about it. I am still retaining hopes but they are slowly diminishing. I am not giving up the idea, but it does not look promising for study over here.

I had a very high compliment paid to me tonight. The M.O. had his teeth cleaned here 10 days ago by one of the dentists, but after seeing my job on Reg, he wanted me to do his over for him, as he said I did such a good job. That coming from one in the medical profession is not bad, I think. The more I can keep my hand in, the better.

Tonight I heard a lecture by Paul Bartel— the French correspondent for the *London Times*— on the Secret Army of France. Bartel is English but has lived all his life in France and was a member of the Foreign Legion. He says that 90% of the population will be with us if we invade; not because we are fighting for the Right, but because they only now realize what life under the Germans is, and know that they will be better off with an Allied victory. This does not include all the French, but a vast majority. He also suggests that France has a secret army of two and a half million men who are armed, if only with rifles. He says that a German named Abetz was most responsible for the downfall of France. Abetz came to Paris as the German Ambassador in 1922 and started immediately to bribe all the Frenchmen he could, knocking the fallacy that it is "the German government and not the German people who caused the war," because Abetz was in Paris long before Hitler came to power. As for "the grand old man, Petain," Bartel says the stories about him at Verdun in the last war are baloney. Foche and Clemenceau both said Petain was a defeatist and a coward, and he only put up a good fight at Verdun because he was threatened, and that otherwise he would have surrendered before the Germans even looked at the place. Whether this was a bit of propaganda or not, I don't know.

It seems funny writing only two pages, but that is the trouble with a typewriter.

Love,

Tom

P.S. What do you think of the typing? (Don't be too harsh; I haven't been at it long.)

Moo and Clive both wish to be remembered to you.

July 21

Dear Mom and Dad,

You say, Mother, that since restrictions in Canada, you cannot make up quite as good parcels, but they sure seem to be. Thanks a lot.

Yesterday they took all our stores away from us which leaves me little to do. I spent most of the afternoon reading dental books, but tonight we had to come back to the clinic to work on the dental records; what a job. I can see names and numbers before my eyes as I write. In the middle of all that, Captain Grayson came in with an officer who had broken his jaw playing ball. We X-Rayed him and dispatched him to the hospital.

We also had a private who woke up one morning and could not

close his mouth; he had been in a brawl some time before, and thought he had a broken jaw. The private went to his M.O., a dirty filthy lousy man, who, among other things, is very lazy, and told him he thought his jaw was broken. The M.O., in his usual fashion, said he wouldn't be able to talk if his jaw was broken and dismissed him without even looking at his face, which was swollen and discoloured. The private let it go. I happened to see him the other day; he was an old patient of ours and told me all about it. So with a "professional interest" (ahem) I told him to come and see us immediately. He came on sick parade the next morning; sure enough, his jaw was broken and partially healed in the wrong position. So we took charge of the case and reported it to the Colonel of the man's unit, who was also a patient of ours. He apparently had been waiting for something like this; he'd been wanting to get rid of his M.O. So we are waiting to see what will happen.

Love,
Tom

August 4
Dear Mom and Dad,
Bob and Trix will have been home and out again by the time you get this. I hope they can stay near each other.

I'd sure appreciate that book *5000 Facts About Canada*. When one is in a foreign country and gets asked questions about Canada, and doesn't know the answers...

It said in last night's paper that sugar and coffee have been rationed in Canada, and that it is worse than over here. We get two ounces of tea a week and as much coffee as we want. It sure will be tough in the Patterson household with only one ounce of tea and four of coffee.

Glad to hear the Rotary Convention was a success, Dad. It must have been good to have so many different races under one roof discussing something constructive instead of destructive.

Glad to hear Tasker is up and about, but he seems forlorn, grumbling continuously; anyway, he means well.

Unofficially, I have been doing a bit of dental work and have been called Doctor more than once. I can't go into detail, but a retired Colonel's wife will be grateful to me for the rest of her life.

I hope to go to London and see the King's dentist this weekend. Mr. Stamp, who knows him, should get a reply to a letter he wrote about me today or tomorrow; my visit hinges on that.

Thursday— Captain Grayson is on leave and the acting C.O. leaves practically everything to me and spends all of his time operating.

There is a new rule that we are not to receive more than 1,000 cigarettes a month; it had to be put into effect because so many fellows were selling them. Cigarettes are now two pence each over here, so there is quite a chance for profit in Canadian ones coming in duty free.

Yesterday Clive got a reply to his letter to Mr. Morris, the King's dentist, saying only, unfortunately, that he is away on holiday and will not be back until the end of August. So I am going to write directly to the Royal College of Dental Surgeons for a syllabus.

In the meantime I am reading every dental magazine I can lay hands on.

This seems like an awful long time to play about and not get anywhere, but when I think of what it will mean if I do get it, it is well worth it. And it can so easily go flop that I want to make absolutely sure of everything first instead of rushing to the first person I meet.

But enough of that.

J.B., who came up with Reg Reid and I to the Stamps', did not prove to be popular. He sat there and ran down the English and was a very good example of the propaganda work of Dr. Goebbels. He finds the English degenerate and lacking guts and initiative, in spite of the work of the R.A.F. and Navy and Commandos. Had he been over here during the Battle of Britain, he would have found he was so wrong, he would be disgusted with himself. But besides the absurdity, it is very rude to talk like that when you are accepting English hospitality. Anyway, he makes a hell of a racket when he eats, which is enough to put anybody off.

When Moo heard about the Canadian tea ration she said she thought she should return the compliment and send some tea to you. Of course, she can't; if she got caught sending food out of the country, she could be charged.

I'm glad to hear you are going to send some hollyhock seed. We have the place picked out for it already. You sow it in the spring, don't you?

Before I forget, can you send a pair of braces over in your next box? The army braces nearly cut your arms off and civilian braces are rationed. So, as the officials say, "This matter may be treated as URGENT."

The news today is very bad. The Germans are going to town in Russia and if it doesn't rain, snow, or sleet soon, things will be terrible.

So long and keep smiling.

Love,

Tom

August 16

Dear Mom and Dad,

I spent last weekend on 48-hour pass at the Stamps'. When I got back to camp Sunday night, I was informed that Grayson, Spell-man— the orderly— and I, were moving on Monday. After 26 months with the same unit, you can imagine my amazement. We were to be ready by noon Monday to proceed to the field.

Quite a bit of my personal stuff was at the Stamps' and I had to collect that and get all the dental equipment packed; quite a job. We got it all done and were ready. As usual, the truck which was to take us did not show up till 8:00 p.m.; we were just a little late getting away.

We had no idea where we were going or anything else. At 9:30 we landed at a little pub in a very little village about the size of Sebringville. The pub was the H.Q. of the Dental Company to which we were going. I wish you could have seen it. Next door to the bar was the lab, and above the pub, the Dental Company and the staff of the pub slept. Our room was next to the barmaid's. There were no locks on any of the doors. When we got up in the morning, we went down the road to an old barn, which was our eating room. Everybody from the C.S.M. to the privates ate there. Then we went back to the stables of the pub, where they had built a sort of washstand down the middle of each manger. There, we shaved etc.

When we went back to our room, the barmaid was walking up and down with her hair in pins and in her dressing gown. She looked lovely, with the shape of a young cow and an expression on her face like a pickaxe.

It was just one big happy family.

We left there at 11:00 and arrived at our final destination about noon. We are now living in an estate of several hundred acres. When we looked out of the back of the truck we saw a beautiful house; one wing is about the size of the Lee's house on William Street. From the main gate to the house is about a mile of windy road through a park. There are hundreds of sheep on each side of the road, and back a little farther are the tents. The house is like a castle and has its own ballroom with a balcony for the orchestra and a huge chandelier in the middle of the ceiling. The front hall is used as the orderly room and for a few other offices. The officers live just above that and the Sergeants live right at the top, in what I imagine is the servants' quarters. There are 68 stairs up to our room. The clinic is in what seems to have been a schoolroom for the estate's children. Right behind the clinic are one pear, one plum, and two apple trees, but it is taking one's life in one's hand to even touch the trees. Right across the road from us is a large stud farm, with several Derby winners etc. on it. Altogether there is £3 million worth of stock, and that is a lot of money. They have one colt worth a cool 60,000 quid or about $300,000. A retired general runs the farm. The owner of this place is a man named Buchanan, the Black & White whiskey man.

The place is beautiful but damned hard to get out of, and there is absolutely nothing to do, though nearly all this week we have been getting settled down. There is very little dentistry work, and when we are finished there is nothing at all to do but walk or sit.

The men have one pail of water per day per tent, and that is for washing, shaving, and drinking. Once a week, a mobile bath calls and stays for a couple of hours. If one of the men happens to be on duty, he is strictly out of luck.

We have a bath in the "Big House" but the room is always so crowded that I have not had a bath since I came here. There are no shows and no canteen. The nearest town is four-and-a-half miles away.

Yesterday afternoon, I went to the Stamps', to see them, take a few things over, and bring others back. It took me three-and-a-half hours to get there, and I had to leave again at 5:30. We get one 48-hour pass a month and that is all. No more short weekends.

Moo had your letter, Mother, and was pleased as punch. She was also worried; you mentioned chicken pox. I hope there was nothing serious. I will write you as soon as I receive your letter.

I took some of the stuff you sent up to the Stamps', so that when I go there on my weekend I'll be able to eat without starving them out of house and home.

Thanks for *Facts About Canada* and the pamphlets.

If you address my mail the same as before, it will get to me okay. I don't think we will be here for very long; we are here so Grayson can get field experience before he gets his majority. I hope we'll be back in our own stall soon; it was much nicer there. (Pardon me while I have a bit of maple sugar which Jimmy has cut for me.) That was good. You sure get good things for your parcels.

Love,

Tom

August 28

Dear Trix and Bob,

I moved about three weeks ago, and it has thrown me all out of kilter as far as letter writing goes (if I ever was in kilter).

But thanks a million for writing.

Trix, you made me homesick starting your letter "Just a-sittin' on the dock." But I hope you are having a good time in Muskoka, and I am glad that Bob and you can be near each other.

You should see the "joint" I am living in. The house has turrets, a wide sweeping staircase and little niches and railings all over the place. When I first saw it all, I felt just like Little Lord Fauntleroy must have felt.

But after the first thrill wears off, one finds that it is still a barracks, and all I do is eat, sleep, and work; I'm in bed by 8:30 or 9:00 every night. There are no newspapers— three radios, that is all.

But it was from this immediate vicinity that the Dieppe raiders started out. It's kind of thrilling that men who were within walking distance made world history. The planes zoom out— and you want to shout, "Give it to 'em." They really fly over in masses. I think the Germans will be pretty unhappy today, too; planes were going out all last night and all today. I have never heard so many before. They have the Battle of Britain beaten.

We are getting a few more raids, but nothing to compare with the ones we are giving them. Occasionally three or four planes come over, but that many hardly ever go back. Then we hear from Germany that some object was attacked and utterly destroyed— some joke.

By the time you get this you will be well on your way to your first wedding anniversary— congratulations and may you have many more under happier circumstances.

Love,
Tom

August 28
Dear Dad and Mom,

Dad, those three pipes are sure lovely but they made me awful mad that I ran out of pipe tobacco about a week ago. I don't want to break them in on cheap cigarette tobacco. The shaving set was very nice— especially the brush. And the food was as good and as welcome as ever. Thanks a lot for the whole works.

How is Don getting along in the army— or is he there yet? Dental Mechanics hold the rank of Sergeant over here, and if they're good, get 75¢ a day trades pay. But I think only veterans are getting that (I mean veteran mechanics).

I think the University of Toronto is running a three-month course in Dental Mechanics for prospective members of the Dental Corps, but I don't know what the qualifications are.

We can't get newspapers or a darn thing here. I've heard rumours that the Russians are driving the Jerries back around Moscow, but are retreating in the south. I hope they can hold on till the winter.

From the Dieppe raid, one can see what a tough job is ahead. I have not spoken to anyone who was there yet, but I know several who did not come back. It was tough fighting.

From incidents since I have come "to the field," I realize the importance of guarding one's conversation. One careless word in public can cost a great many lives.

We are getting more air raids now, but nothing to be worried about. One or two planes sneak in— and they don't stay very long, or else they stay forever. On Wednesday night, three planes came over and only one went back.

But our planes are going over 24 hours a day.

It must be hell over there. I have never heard so many planes, Spitfires to four-engined bombers, English, Canadian, and American. It is really nice to see them all flying fast and low. But the Germans won't think they look so nice.

I am working hard on getting the dental course— but I am in a hole... Until I was moved, I could get time off whenever I wanted, within reason (on weekends, etc.), but here I get one weekend a month. I expect an interview with Mr. Morris, the King's dentist, some time soon, but I do not want Grayson to know about it or he will try and horn in and get me to introduce him so he can "steal the show." I am not for it. He boasts that he will meet the Queen and tell her about the filling in her front tooth before he leaves England. He'd be mad if he knew what I was planning and am keeping from him.

My programme is to see Mr. Morris, for information and prestige with Canadian dentists; I am going to try and get him to refer me officially to the Royal College of Dental Surgeons. I'll see what they have that I will have a chance to take. Then I'm going to the Educational Officer at C.M.H.Q., who can arrange time off for me to study, and from him I'll work through to Colonel Lott of the Dental Corps, who is also a professor at U. of T. This is what I plan; the whole thing may alter for better or worse with one word from Mr. Morris. Please keep your fingers crossed.

And I guess *I'd* better not talk too much before I know definitely what is to be done.

Love,
Tom

September 29

Dear Mom and Dad,

That sounds like quite an interesting ceremony you took part in at the commissioning of the minesweeper, and I'll bet the men were really happy to receive all that you gave them. I hope they have the best of luck. I hope you don't think I'm rude in asking, but is the city going to keep in touch with the men? Over here, a small village or a city will often adopt a boat of some kind and keep in touch with all the personnel. I know the men would appreciate it, and it would be a way of dragging people in who have no direct interest in the war, like old people with no children, or school kids.

How are your feet, Dad? I hope by the time you get this you will be up and around as if nothing had happened. I guess it was pretty painful. Hope you won't have any more trouble with them.

Mrs. Stamp received her birthday box and was very pleased; and she did not have to pay any duty on it. As far as I know, there is nothing like that over here and no talk of it.

About the only thing I really need in the line of clothes is socks. I have sleeveless sweaters and the one turtleneck, and still have enough underwear and lots of handkerchiefs. You could put a bar of soap or soap flakes in every second parcel, though. We get soap coupons which entitle us to one bar of washing soap (Lifebuoy, etc.) or one tupenny (4¢) box of Lux. How quickly we use up such small bits.

Bob sure seems to be getting on okay. They are going to be a long distance from you, but it is still better than sending him out of the country and separating them.

You make my mouth water when you talk of corn. How I would like some right now. My corn was a failure. The ground is not good for corn; in fact, it is rotten. And we had a very wet summer. So it grew to be 9" tall— 196 plants— and then stood still.

A few shops are selling corn, but it is eight pence a cob, and none of it is good. Back home they'd be ashamed to feed that stuff to cattle.

Sometimes, hearing of all these fellows getting their commissions makes me think what a dope I was not to join up with a fighting unit. But then I realize that in spite of the money, I am probably getting more out of it than them and still doing my duty, so I shouldn't kick. In the Dental Corps you have to have your degree before you can get your commission, and by the look of things that is going to be almost impossible, though I haven't given up hope. I don't know whether Mr. Morris is sick or what, but he has not answered Clive's letter. Of course, he is a very old man and is more or less "resting on his laurels." So there still may be a chance.

Nevertheless I am studying, and last weekend Captain Gray bought me two books— one on extractions and the other a medical dictionary— both very useful. And I read all the dental journals from cover to cover. But the best way I have struck so far is talking to people. Some fellow asks me about a certain thing and I explain it to him the best way I know how— but they always ask questions in such a way that I find something new I don't know, and I make a point of finding it out. That may sound a bit muddled but you know what I mean.

The smoke and cheers and tears of the Dieppe raid have died away and some details are coming out. The Dieppe troops were from this district and I've talked to a couple of them. They seem to think it was well worthwhile and are anxious to go back again. That convoy they met put the whole thing on the rocks, at least as far as the casualties were concerned. It alerted the Germans that something was happening, so they could prepare; and the convoy delayed one landing party about 15 minutes, which threw everything out of gear. But at a lecture the officers were given, the authorities seemed pleased with the results, although they were not counting on such a large casualty list.

One fellow who was there said, "If nothing else, it proved we can take and hold any part of the coast for any length of time."

One regiment, though, went over with 80 men and came back with 127. The extras had gone A.W.O.L. the night before and stowed away on the barges. They weren't for missing anything.

By the way, the censors are getting really strict. Within the last month four soldiers received two-year sentences "for making known the disposition and location of His Majesty's forces." Two years is a long long time to spend in one place.

Glad to hear Barney is keeping so well. I was beginning to wonder if he was dead and you hadn't said anything. But I hope he holds out till I get back, and from the sound of things, he will.

The Stamps have been hit pretty hard financially from the war, and England is no place for a middle-aged man to start afresh, so they are all het up about going to Canada after the war. Mrs. Stamp likes the idea of a hotel in Muskoka. She would like to get a job in a big hotel for a year, get on the inside of the business, and then try and get a hotel of her own. I think it a very good idea; Canada is definitely the country of the future, and Muskoka is really just opening up. What do you think?

Happy Birthdays to you both and I hope by this time next year you will be able to celebrate in peace. Sorry you had to spend your day in bed, Dad, but I'm glad you're better.

Love,

Tom

October 1

Dear Mom,

I hardly know what to say, Mother. I hope you will not misunderstand me, and will excuse my lack of words.

I received Phyl's first telegram Friday morning 25-9-42, although it was sent at the beginning of the week. The last telegram came through on Saturday afternoon.

Saturday morning I telephoned Colonel Blair and asked him if I could get leave to travel to Canada by air. He said that any leave was out of the question; C.M.H.Q. would turn it down flat.

But, Mom, believe me that I was with you in thought, as I still am. I long for something to happen that could send me back to Canada on a course or some other Godsend.

Somehow, Mom, I can't think of anything to say that sounds right. I hope that Dad did not suffer at all and that he went with pleasant memories of us all. He is probably much better off than he has been for some time. I think he has been frightened of this for the last few years if not longer. But you will probably have all that settled in your own mind by the time you get this, so I won't say anything more about it.

Bob will be discharged now, won't he? Please write as soon as you can and let me know everything.

Right from the first telegram I have felt so helpless that sometimes I wanted a pair of wings.

I was at the Stamps' on Saturday afternoon; I'd left word with the Signal Office to telephone any messages through. Moo took the message and broke the news to me. I got three days' compassionate leave and spent it with the Stamps. I shall never be able to thank them enough for the home they have given me.

Mother, this letter seems to be a flop from start to finish but I know if I wrote it over it would be the same if not worse. I think I better close and will write when I hear from you again.

All my love,
Tom

October 8
Dear Mom,

Mom, we have moved again. We are still attached to the same unit, but now that we are "in the field" we will be moving all over the place.

We are now living in Eric Coates' summer home; is the sea air ever nice. You sense it a couple of miles away and when you get right near the ocean— why, there is all the difference in the world. We will probably be here for the winter. The house is nice, but not nearly as big as the mansion we were in. There are wash basins in our rooms, though, and only two sleeping in my room. Five of us live here together. Downstairs in the two front rooms are our clinic and the M.O.'s, and we have our own kitchen with a hot water system and stove. The M.O.'s staff has one room and Spellman, my orderly, and I have the other. The third is a sick bay for minor things such as flu, colds etc. There is also a bath, which makes everything very nice.

Eventually we will be cooking for ourselves, but for the present we are eating with the Quartermaster stores, so we should do all right.

I have not had much of a chance to look around yet, but it looks like a large edition of Grand Bend.

Two hundred yards down the street from us, right on the sea front, is a big hotel, which was built by Clive's father's butler. After old Mr. Stamp died, the butler had enough money to build this hotel and is supposed to have made a fortune out of it.

I was going to send this letter air mail, but air mail is sure to be censored, so I'll send it through regular channels. I don't think I've said anything I shouldn't have— but just in case.

I am sorry I got you excited about that promotion, which might have come had things remained the way they were. But when Grayson moved, everything changed.

I don't know, but this last summer seems to have been one of disappointment after disappointment.

Everything seems to have gone wrong.

My course didn't come through. Mr. Morris is sick or something and hasn't answered any letters at all. Clive's mother, an old friend of his, did not even get an answer on a personal matter, so I don't know what is wrong.

But I guess that is the way it goes and one of these days my luck will change.

One night just before I left the other place, I was in the canteen watching a show, and a Sergeant asked me if I could relieve a lady of a toothache. I said yes, and after the show, I went over to the clinic and extracted one tooth and then took out the root of another tooth. She was one of the workmen's wives. I went around to see her the next day and she was so pleased, she said she wanted two more teeth pulled and that I was the only one she wanted to do it. She said I was the best dentist she'd ever been to. But by the look of her mouth, I don't think she had seen many dentists before, if any. She then recommended another girl who was suffering toothache to me. This one was quite young and very nervous. But I got it out and she was pleased with the job.

Her family were evacuees from the East End of London. They had been through all the big blitzes and the old lady was the "Mrs. Minerva" type. They invited me in to evening tea and I sat around their cottage with all the kids and the whole family. For tea— about 10:00 p.m.— they served bread and margarine, cheese, tomatoes, beet root, and tea. (He worked in a lumber mill, so he got an extra ration of cheese.) They were very nice in a simple sort of way. I'm not being snobbish; the average working class person over here doesn't know the score on anything.

I am glad you got Mrs. Stamp's letter. She was beginning to worry. She wrote you last week, air mail, so you should get mine and hers about the same time.

What is King doing about conscription? If he doesn't hurry up he will have a hell of a mess on his hands. The only ones left to be conscripted will be the yellow ones.

King's casualty list of Dieppe was propaganda. I don't know what for, but it was not true. There were men listed as wounded who had no more than a scratch and were giving a Commando exhibition a week later. Some think King was trying to make it look as though the English made the Canadians take the dirty end of it. I heard from pretty good authority that the casualty list for the whole force— English, Canadian, and Russian— was only as large as the one King gave out for Canadians alone.

I am sorry, Mom, but there is one hell of an argument going on in this room and I can't think or do anything else. So I guess I'd better close and continue tomorrow when the air is a little less frigid and more quiet. So goodnight for now.

Good morning.

Things are much quieter now.

How is the quilting coming along— or have you given it up for a while? You seem to have done your fair share, but I think it would be good to have somebody in to keep you company.

Mother, don't you worry about not being useful. Your quilts, socks, pyjamas etc. relieve some younger person who could do work you may not be able to. This is a total war and everyone is in it. Over here, if a girl is excused from leaving home on medical grounds, she has to take the place of another girl— a maid to an invalid, for instance. Everyone helps— if not directly then by taking the place of someone who can act directly.

But sometimes I feel the same way. I get the urge to whack at them directly— but then you see men with a toothache, or trench mouth, etc. and realize that they have to be fixed up; they know more about fighting etc. than I do.

But enough of that. It must be noisy in Stratford with trucks, trains, airplanes and riveters. But as you say— you are not bothered with bombing or blackouts which are more interfering now, and so can turn out so much more.

Keep your chin up.

Love,
Tom

October 14
Dear Mom,
They've inaugurated a new Air Mail Service; we are allowed four per month. Let me know how long this takes to reach you, will you?

We are still in the same place and just getting to know our way around. It is quiet, but our quarters are comfortable and we eat very well. So that is a lot.

On account of the petrol shortage, all our correspondence with H.Q. is coming by mail instead of Dispatch Rider, but if it helps to shorten the war, it is all to the good.

Last night I called at a fisherman's to get some lobster. They invited me in and I sat and talked to them for a couple of hours. He was the real old fisherman type and they were both as religious as they make them. They were very nice and gave me a drink and some books to take back to our cottage.

I wanted to get the lobsters for next weekend when I'll visit the Stamps, to help out with the meals; it will also be quite a treat for them. Lobsters are practically impossible to get inland and sell at an exorbitant price.

So, barring gunfire, stormy weather, the Admiralty and about

50 other things, I am going to get some lobster. These fishermen are really marvellous. This one was bombed out a short while ago; he just moved to another house and carried on. Nothing makes them give in.

I got Moo to send you some flowers for me at a shop I found. I hope they got to you okay. She wanted to send some herself, but found she was not allowed; it was just for the troops.

What do you think of the shackling of prisoners by the Germans? The people over here are up in arms about it, but nobody seems to know what to do, and nobody wants to end up in a race to see who can do the worst.

All the time I have been writing this, there has been gunfire out in the Channel; it is in the distance and may only be practice.

There is activity down here day and night, most of it a long way off. Occasionally we see a convoy going through with their barrage balloons and air escort.

I'd better close; we have just been called to pay parade and I can post this there.

Love,
Tom

October 21
Dear Mom,
We used to have our mail delivered by the same truck that brings our supplies, but now they send stores, lab work, and all by Field Post Office because of the petrol shortage. And you know what happens with every change, especially in the army.

This will be short, Mother; I am feeling as blue as hell. Nothing in particular is wrong— just one of those spells.

I will be glad when this bloody war is over and I can go back to ordinary living and not have to cater to guys like Grayson. He hasn't got a sane thought in his head, and conducts himself like a child of three.

But enough of that. Talking about it doesn't do any good.

We've had a few delicacies in the food line; last night we had some shrimps as a "midnight" snack (about 9:30 p.m.). And this morning I got up early and picked mushrooms at a farm on the outskirts of the town.

This afternoon, I felt that if I did not get away I would go nuts. I had the afternoon off and went to the Stamps', a long trip but well worth it. Moo cooked the mushrooms and I had them on toast for supper. They cost about 7/6 a pound over here, about $1.75, so you know what a delicacy they are.

In camp about 10 of us eat together; we'll also have Grayson next week. Five of the fellows belong to the Quartermaster's stores, so we will not starve. But the noises and conversation that go on during meals are enough to drive a guy crazy. Grayson is as bad as any of them and eats like a pig. But there I go again.

I'd better fold up for tonight and will write again next week. Don't worry about my state of mind too much; it helps to get it off my chest.

Mom, keep fighting in there.

Lots of love,
Tom

October 23

Dear Phyl,

We are in one of those fishing towns where there is no fishing in the winter time— you know the kind.

But it is much better than the last place; there are two pubs 100 yards up the street, and a cinema. Our cottage has good central heating and is very comfortable.

All in all, we are very lucky, and I still get up to see Moo at least once a week and sometimes more.

I have met a fisherman's family here; they are characters. Their house is spotless and they themselves are clean and religious. But the old man is the type poems are written about. Last night he was sitting on the floor, peeling canes to make his lobster baskets out of for today. It makes you want to be able to paint. He is about 64, with tousled dark grey hair, and he sits there with his horn-rimmed glasses on the tip of his nose, whittling away, taking all the bumps off about 100 willow canes. You must think I've gone artistic or something from the way I am talking. Maybe it is the atmosphere here.

We get a few air-raid warnings, but nothing happens. Almost every day we see our planes going over the Channel to France, but there is seldom any sign of Jerries.

How are you getting along? It seems months since I've heard from you or Mom, but I guess it is because I have wanted news so much.

Love,
Tom

October 27
Dear Bob and Trix,

I guess you think I am quite a heel, not writing for so long. Please pardon me. I will try to do better. I have had no mail for so long that I almost forget how to answer a letter. Every day I go over to the Field Post Office and watch them sorting the letters— everybody else's!

Everything has been on the move so much here that there is a general mix-up all round.

Grayson is right in his glory, but it is a pretty good posting when you think of where we could be.

The cottage is not big enough for the M.O. and D.O., so I think they are going to requisition another house and put us in it.

Last weekend the Milan and Genoa raiders passed directly over us— at least 50 of them. More will be going over tonight, as it is beautiful and clear and the R.A.F. hardly ever miss now.

Yesterday was lousy. It poured rain and the wind blew a small gale.

We are having "nuisance" or "reprisal" raids, whichever you want to call them, but never more than one or two raiders in one place and they always pick a cloudy day. A huge difference from two years ago!

The Egyptian affair has started again, but General Montgomery seems a hell of a good man. He was our G.O.C. before going to Egypt, and everyone who had anything to do with him admires him. He is a Dr. Jackson man— gets up at 7:30 and takes everything along with the men. And there is no fooling with him.

I expect you are out of the army now, Bob. I hope so. Please write soon and tell me how Mom is and what is going on. I have received almost no mail since the telegram saying that Dad died.

I can hardly believe it even yet.

I hope everything is okay and that Mom is okay. Please write as soon as you can and let me know.

As ever,

Tom

October 28

Dear Mom,

Thanks for your most welcome air mail letter.

I am glad, Mother, that Dad went with so little pain, and as you say, it is much better than partially recovering and having to stay in bed for the rest of his life.

I think it is what he would have liked. I am sorry that he did not receive my letter acknowledging his parcel, though. I thought of that as soon as I got your first telegram. It was hard when I realized there was nothing I could do for him or you. I did hope that he had received my letter.

I am glad Bob could get home so soon, but I wish he could get out of the army altogether. I suppose we cannot ask for too much, though. It was good of the bank to let Phyl off, too, and I am glad she could be with you.

How is the business going? Don't you take on too much all at once. It is brave of you to go into the office and get to know the business, and I hope you are getting along okay.

It was funny of Dad leaving no will. He never would say anything about that. I hope you are well looked after, though, and that you will not have anything to worry about.

Mother, I am sorry that I could not be with you during all the trouble, and I'm glad Phyl and Don were so good and helped you so much. I was with you in spirit just the same. I tried to fly to you but of course there was not a chance. I had to sit and wish. Mom, as you say, the only way to look at it is that it was all for the best.

I am glad you got Moo's letters. Did you get the flowers?

Mom, goodnight for now...

Love,
Tom

November 10

Dear Mom,

My leave has come and gone quietly; I did not have exactly an overflow of money, and I didn't feel like doing much anyway.

The Captain is getting harder and harder to work with. Sometimes I think I will blow up and bust, but so far I've managed to keep my temper. Back at the old camp, I could get away from it all at night, but now he is with me 24 hours a day. He is even talking about sleeping at the clinic with us.

During my leave I went to London, to the Royal Dental Hospital and the Examination Hall, to enquire about a course. They could give me nothing but a full four-year course, which, of course, I cannot take. So that is that.

When I returned, Gray told me he had been to see Colonel Lott and found out that Lott has written to the Dean of the Faculty of Dentistry at U. of T. about me. What the outcome will be, I do not know, but I'm hoping for the best.

There were no letters from home when I got back from leave, but 1,000 cigarettes from Dad which had been posted September 10.

One of the reasons for the mail hold-up is the shipping diverted to North Africa, I think. I could almost go without any mail if the space can always be used to such advantage.

People over here have taken a new lease on life. The defeat of Rommel would have cheered anyone up, but the American landings on top of that—

Planes are always going over to Occupied France; a thrilling and beautiful sight. Yesterday there were 100 bombers and fighters flying over, 10 feet above the housetops. From everywhere to the north came squadrons of planes, and the air was vibrating with them.

I hope, Mom, that you are getting my letters, and Mrs. Stamp's. I will never be able to repay them for all they have done, especially in the last month or so.

Lots of love,
Tom

November 12
Dear Mom,

You mentioned the pictures Reg Reid sent home— well, although I look almost bald in them, it is more because my hair is unphotogenic than anything else.

I am very glad that everyone has been so kind to you. Fred Maples seems to have been a Godsend, and he is an awfully good man to have as a helper, too. But Mom, you have been so good that it is coming back now.

I don't think I am too thin. I have lost four pounds since leaving home, but the weight will come back in no time once I get eating good food and living settled. Almost everyone in England has lost weight in the last three years.

I am sorry to hear about Don's ear, but tell him he is very lucky to go into the factory. He would not like it over here, and besides, he can do a lot there, both for the country in producing munitions, and for you.

I hope your trip to Toronto provided you with a rest; you must have been almost a nervous wreck, doing all that had to be done.

Everyone over here has had a weight lifted from their minds. The Germans are having their numbers very quickly lowered; and because they have taken over the whole of France, they'll be weakened on the northern coast. It looks very much like the French fleet will come over to the United Nations, which would clarify a lot. But it is almost useless to write of these events; they are moving so rapidly. Today's news is tomorrow's history.

Ham has really been getting on my nerves. He is one of the most ignorant, stupid men I have ever met. I heard about his wife going to Toronto, which does not please him in the least. But I try not to think of him, whenever I can.

I've received a number of them, but I hate writing replies to letters of condolence; it's so hard to say the right thing. But I will write them.

Love,
Tom

November 25
Dear Mom,
Am writing in pencil because there's so little ink; and besides, what there is has already been watered down three times.

Saturday afternoon, after I'd finished a bit of work, I was standing at the window, starting to pour a model, when I heard a queer whizzing. I looked up and saw a black streak coming through the air, apparently straight at us. You can imagine how fast I was down on the floor. Anyway— a practice shell had fallen short, went through the back of the house next to us, came out the side wall, and buried itself just below our building. The bricks and plaster from the other house came through our windows, and in one room broke every bit of glass. Jimmy Spellman was in that room but only received a slight cut on his hand. Brick pieces the size of fists flew through the two rooms Jimmy and I were in, but neither of us were hurt in the least.

So I did not write you then.

Sunday I went up to the Stamps'. Clive is a Captain in the

Regular Army now, but attached to a Home Guard Battalion as Adjutant. He is away practically all the time, but they will move nearer his H.Q. The Stamps are very unsettled; Clive has only been at his new posting two weeks, and does not know quite how the land lies.

I know he'd appreciate it very much if you congratulated him in your next letter.

Monday about 3:30, Colonel Blair and Colonel Climo visited us. Colonel Blair is being moved and Climo, a Halifax man, is taking his place. No one is particularly pleased, but that's the way it goes.

Colonel Blair brought me a dental textbook to study, so I spent Monday night with it.

Tuesday we had a big inspection, and here it is, Wednesday afternoon.

The papers yesterday and today are full of the Russian news. Maybe we will be home for next Christmas. Whatever one thinks of the Russians, they sure can fight, and are getting rid of a lot of Germans; and our forces in North Africa are taking everything in stride. The R.A.F. is pounding on as usual. We may be in action somewhere soon. But one never knows; and I don't want to give the censor a chance to earn his money.

We have the Germans on the run now, and the only way to beat them decisively is to keep them that way. I don't see how he can possibly go on in Russia, Egypt, Tunis, and keep his large army of occupation strong enough to hold down all of Europe.

But we have to wait and see.

I'm glad you think Moo's idea of running a hotel is a good one. I think with her looks, personality, and Englishness, if you know what I mean, they could really put it over. About that course in hotel management, do you think she could take it by correspondence over here? Let me know if it could be arranged, or better yet, write Moo and tell her.

You certainly seem to be doing a fine job on the quilts; it's hardly believable that only two women could make so many.

Seems as though everybody over there is either married or getting married. Ted and Hilda Tomlinson are going to have a baby. This may be a secret, but I got the letter from Ted the other day and you would die laughing at the way he puts things. But don't let on I told you.

I am going to have clam straight from the sea at the fisherman's tonight. Keep smiling.

Love,
Tom

December 9

Dear Mom,

I will send some pictures when I can, but they are very hard to get now. Did you ever receive my letter asking for a cheap camera? If you could send one of those small Brownies and a few films, I could get a lot more snaps. It is practically impossible to get film now, and the few cameras are as expensive as h———.

I have almost given up getting any dental courses until after the war, although I am still studying and putting in my plug where I can. The Dental Officers jockey around so much among themselves that they have no time for a Sergeant, and I haven't a very good man working for me. He pulls about as much weight as my little finger, though I think he has been told off; he's settled down a bit.

Mom, I have to thank you for bringing me up so that I love my home, yet when I'm away from it, I don't act childishly.

I hope you aren't overworking yourself. You must feel very tired and strained after all you've been through, but I hope you are okay. It will be nice for you, having Phyl home every weekend. I wish I could do the same.

How long is Bob going to be home? I knew he was trying to get leave, and am awfully glad he got it.

It does make a difference knowing that you are secure. I only hope the succession duty men do not get too "grabby."

Mom, Phyl and Harry are really in love. I wish you could read the letters Harry sends me; they'd make you laugh.

People here are preparing for peace, but it is as though they are passing through a kind of revolution— as only England can. The war has hit some classes very hard. The lower classes have a kind of "emancipation" which they cannot quite live up to, the lower middle classes are doing better than anyone else financially, the upper middle classes are stranded, and the upper classes are divided in two— those with money, and those without. The whole thing boils down to education. The lower classes send their children to the "Council" schools which hardly teach the three "Rs."

The lower middle classes— shopkeepers, etc., are receiving more money and yet they can still give their children free education and do not have to live up to very much.

The upper middle class, which is just under the aristocracy, pays through the nose for everything. They educate their children at "Public School," which costs a fortune. If they are not educated there, they do not even speak the same language as their parents. Consequently, they have few children. Few of them have any money left.

The upper classes are okay as long as they have money, but without it can do nothing. The Stamps have a friend who owned a castle in the north; before the Depression it was a thriving community. Queen Mary used to go there for tea and visits. After the Depression, the family's mother died and the boy took over. The tenants had been there as long as the Wurmolds, but couldn't pay any rent. The boy told the Stamps, "What can I do, they belong there as much as I do. I can't turn them out." And so the tenants went on living there, rent free, while he lived in one room in London. Eventually he had to sell the estate to an American. That's the way one of the families that made England died out.

Since Bob and Trix are at home, I will thank them again for their lovely Christmas present. Thanks a million. As soon as I get back I will return it with a wedding present.

I have to clean the teeth of one of the technicians now, so I will close.

Love,
Tom

December 18
Dear Mom,
Thanks for the onions and the cigarettes and tobacco; all was especially appreciated. I had just run out when they came, so thank Trix for the cigarettes and thank you for the tobacco.

I am going up to the Stamps' tomorrow and will take the package wrapped in Christmas paper with me unopened, along with some of the other things.

On Tuesday the boss had sciatica so badly he had to go into sick bay for a couple of days. What a relief. I had an awful lot of work to do, but a few days' rest from him was pleasant. He's getting worse— and then he wonders why he doesn't get his promotion. I told him the other day that he looked absolutely disgraceful. The one decent battle dress he's got, he has his crowns on. A bit premature, don't you think? But his other one is worse than the privates' fatigue clothes. Nobody likes him except a few tarts.

So if I blow up one of these days, don't be surprised; I might tell him exactly what I think of him. He won't be able to do anything about it because he knows deep down that it is true. He really has got me down and if it wasn't for the education I am getting I would have told him where to get off long ago. But enough of that.

1943 should be a big year, and at last the Canadians will have something to talk about. That is another point where the boss's true character shows— he is as yellow as a canary's wing. Only a few pretend to have no fears at all, but most of the fellows look at what has to be done as what has to be done, and they do it. He is the kind who says it has to be done, but let somebody else go to it (until they start dishing out the praise).

Mrs. Stamp is sending you some flowers for Christmas, but they will have my name on them as she is not allowed to do it. Moo and Clive send their best.

All my love,
Tom

December 29
Dear Mom,

Well, it is after Christmas. By this time next year, I hope I will be able to recall writing this letter to you in person. Maybe that's wishful thinking, but no harm done.

I had a lovely Christmas, the best since I have been in England. I stayed at the Stamps' from Thursday till Sunday; I was very lucky.

Christmas morning, I brought tea into the Stamps' bedroom and surprised them with Christmas presents for them in a stocking. They were very pleased. My Christmas present from them is coming as soon as we can get out together to a bookstore; they are going to give me a book and want to make sure that I will like it.

All Christmas Day we lay around. About 6:30 some officers billeted across the road from the Stamps came in for dinner, a darned good bunch from St. Thomas. One of them knew Trix, but I did not catch his name and did not want to appear rude.

For dinner we had a lovely goose— from Clive's sister— with a really delicious meal— we had been saving up for it for quite a while. The fruit that you sent over, plus a bit more, was given to a baker who baked us a really nice cake. He thought we were being too extravagant, so only put half the fruit in the cake and returned the rest. Nevertheless, it was very good.

We also managed to scrounge a bit of drink, which is as scarce as hens' teeth.

On Christmas Day one of Moo's chickens came through with her first two eggs. Apparently, she made a special effort for Christmas; she has done nothing since.

Back in camp on Sunday night I had three letters from you, one from Phyl and several Christmas cards waiting for me; that was as good as any Christmas present could have been.

Mom, my letters lately have been pretty blue, but don't pay any attention. It was one of those times when everything seemed to go wrong. I've made up my mind that the boss isn't going to worry me any more; I'll just stay out of his way as much as I possibly can and make the best of it when I am with him. He is a hopeless case; there is no use worrying about it. For the first two days of my scheme this has worked very well.

I am glad you liked the English airmen you had to the house. Mom, don't think that the R.A.F. are bad or anything like that. It is the same over here. A few Canadians go wild for one night and it takes the rest of the regiment a month to break down all the sorry reputation those fellows built up. Some of these men are away from home for the first time, and a few are bound to go haywire, especially stationed at Port Albert.

Glad to hear that Bob has his six months' leave. It sure will be a help to all concerned.

Right now it is as black as hell out; the minute you step outside the door you bump into something. There are hardly any women left here and the ones that are, are lousy. In the morning we are supposed to get up in the blackout and walk 1/4 of a mile to breakfast— but we never go. We scrounge some bread etc. and have something ourselves. There is no heat in the mornings, and when those old sea breezes blow, it's really cold. Even our beds with iron slats feel comfortable then.

I'm glad you like these letters, Mom, and that you've kept them.

Sorry I can't keep your letters; over here we have so little room to carry so much that I can't do it, especially moving around the way I am these days.

Love,
Tom

— 1943 —

January 19

Dear Mom,

Someone sure made a "faux pas," putting matches in that overseas parcel, eh? Anything I had in that fire must have been burnt. Parcels and letters were coming through in pretty bad shape, but even those have stopped now.

Some English-Canadian mail was lost around November 1st, and I posted my Christmas cards then. I'm glad some of them got through, but, as you say, the ships are on much more important missions than carrying mail.

Today I sent a cable asking for money. I hope you don't mind. I really hate doing it, but my leave came suddenly. It may be my last leave for a while, and I badly want to get away from this life I am leading, if only for a week.

The place I am in now is much the same as Grand Bend, with the same kind of people. It is about the most immoral place I've been posted yet. I suppose I shouldn't say that; so many of the villagers have been called up that it is hard to judge from the men remaining here; many of them should be in the Services, but are evading it quite legally. That is about all one can say.

And I can also truthfully say that I have not been out with one girl since I arrived here. They are all a bunch of "worn out" crocks.

I think you will remember Doctor Smith saying once how men need women to keep them on a level keel— well, he was perfectly right, and this war is no exception. Don't think I'm becoming a prig or an old man, but if I went out to "enjoy" myself like the average youth over here, I would have to knock all my brains out first and begin again as someone else.

And now that the women are being called up as fast as the men, it is clear that they need men just as badly as men need them.

Don't think that I mean all the women over here are tarts or anything. It's just that the good ones are hard to get at, and by the time you wade through the others, you would rather have stayed in your barracks and read a book.

But enough of that.

I have not received your parcel with the Vitamin C or the cod-liver oil, but I hope I get it soon; my head is plugged up almost constantly. As soon as the longer days start, I'll be able to get more exercise, unlike now; I'm pinned down with work.

How is that steelworkers' strike going? They should conscript the whole damn lot of them and make them work on soldiers' pay. The guys over here are sore as the devil about that strike coming just at a time when everybody needs to put in extra effort to shorten this war. How I would like to address a public meeting of those strikers. They would probably mob me, but not before I told them what I thought.

Lots of love,

Tom

P.S. I forgot to tell you that last Friday I went to the hospital for a chest X-Ray which turned out negative for T.B.— so I am okay.

P.P.S. You remember the officers I mentioned, that the Stamps had for Christmas? Well, one of them turned up last week and was very apologetic. Mrs. Stamp said she thought he really meant it. He stayed for a couple of hours.

A Routine Order I wrote four months ago about trench mouth has just officially appeared. I wrote it as a local order for our unit— and we sent it in to our H.Q. with our Progress Report. Then it was sent up to London and adopted as a Routine Order C.A. (Overseas). Getting into the big stuff, eh?

But that is all for now. I fooled myself by leaving your letter unsealed to see if I could think of any of the things I missed— and it worked.

Love,
Tom

January 26
Dear Mom,

From the news today it appears as though big things are in the making. I expect they are; that is why I want this leave to be a good one. But we behave here as if everything is going on as usual.

Moo got your letter along with the cheque, and of course she was very pleased to hear from you. But she commented on your still using "Mrs. Stamp." In England, once you are friends with people it is kind of unfriendly to use formal titles. The old saying is— once in an Englishman's home, you are one of the family.

Once again, thanks a million for the leave cheque. I will write soon; let me know how long this takes to reach you.

Love,
Tom

February 12

Dear Mom,

I hope you have received my air-graph letters and in good time. I was so busy I thought I'd better let you know I am still here.

About my leave... The first few days I spent at the Stamps'. It was quiet, but everything here is, and it was such a pleasant change to get away and to be out in the open all day. We went for meals at hotels, took long walks, and generally had a lazy-dazy time of it. Then Clive went on a course, so Moo and I stayed with Moo's mother at Arpington Kent, a suburb of London and the usual type of town built onto a large city. They moved there to get out of the raids and yet be near London.

We went up to London several times and saw a couple of good shows— *Orchestra Wives* with Glenn Miller— and as Moo had never seen *Gone with the Wind* we went to that— and I was very pleased to see it again. Surprising difference what a few years makes in one's knowledge. I got far more out of the movie this time than when I saw it in Stratford.

At the Piccadilly Hotel we had hors d'oeuvres, lamb (one slice), potatoes (baked), and beans. For dessert, a "ba-ba," which is plain cake with rum and butter sauce over it— at least that's what it is in wartime. The price was 6/6d each, or about $1.60. This is a good hotel; in all the restaurants the meals are just as plain as that now.

We had wine with the meal, too. They palmed some not so good stuff on me— not that the price was exorbitant or anything like that— but I don't think they would have done it if I hadn't been Canadian, and if I knew wines.

When the waiter came around with the bill, we complained, and Moo, who knows a bit more about it than I, but not much as she lets on— Clive usually does the choosing— did the talking.

When the waiter found out that he was not pulling the wool over our eyes, he changed his accent from French to ordinary East End Cockney. He apologized and became very friendly.

Clive got the weekend off and came down, too. Saturday night we all sat around and talked about the war. Sunday, Moo's brother came home. I think I have told you before that he is quite a bigshot in the movies— lunch with Noel Coward, etc., etc. Anyway, he was called up and spent several months as an A.C.Z. in training. He was getting along quite well and even made some trips over enemy territory in a bomber when they called him back to the studio and he got his own cutting room, bedroom and everything else back again. He is getting Sergeant's pay now instead of big money. He is doing a lot of secret work, like the Churchill tours, Dieppe raid and all types of films which have to wait to be released.

I returned Sunday night a happier and better man.

This week has been more or less a mix-up. First of all we had to get organized. Monday was okay, but on Tuesday the reaction set in and neither Gray nor myself felt like working— nevertheless, we stuck it out. Wednesday the regiment went on a shoot and they just got back tonight, so our parades were very small; but whenever I started to do something, someone came in or phoned. I couldn't seem to get organized. This morning I did manage to get nearly all my washing done— and as soon as I finish this I am going to have a bath.

But how are you getting along? I'm so glad you had a pleasant Christmas. I know it is pretty quiet, but it is that way everywhere, so until this b—— war is cleaned up I guess we have to put up with it.

How bad is it with those hoarders? They should be put in jail, I think. But then there are always people who think only of themselves. In fact, I think that is one of the main causes of this war.

That sounds like a lovely party you had on New Year's Day. I'm glad my flowers arrived in time. It was a good way to get over the day, and to return people's kindnesses. But Mom, you deserve them all, or else they would have left you flat— as many people do when one is in trouble.

As for letters, on average we have been very lucky. Moo's stepfather, who is a censor, was surprised when I told him that I was receiving most of my mail about a month after it was posted. He said they usually take much longer than that.

It is a funny thing, but the fellows from Stratford over here very seldom meet. It is the same with everybody, no matter where they come from. No one hardly bothers to look anyone else up; it is so hard to make arrangements for meetings, etc.— even though we are only a short distance apart. I don't now what it is, but something seems to change people when they get in the army and they just live from day to day instead of going to the bother of a lot of planning. This sounds very muddled but it is a hard thing to explain because it is so queer.

The other day a Stratfordite *did* look me up. Don should know him; he is a photographer named King. He married a girl from the village I am stationed in and was home not too long ago on leave.

Moo received your letter a short time ago and will answer it soon. She is very busy with the chickens, the housework, Savings Group etc. etc. I know she would love to get a parcel from you, Mom. Toilet soap, Lux, noodle soup, tinned corn, tinned fruit (peaches, etc.), jam, tinned meat, sandwich spread, semi-sweetened chocolate (I forget the name, but it is the same brand as the unsweetened chocolate you use. I wish you would send me some, too— it is darn good in an emergency), greasy face cream (as greasy as possible), and khaki socks for Clive. This sounds like an auction sale or something, but I am giving you the whole works so you can choose— oh, yes, Moo's brother asked me if it was at all possible to get an electric razor for him. If you could get it out of my money, we could fix it up over here. I don't know whether they are still on the market over there or not.

Mom, you suggested in one of your letters that I should give the Stamps up. I don't think you really meant that. If it had not been for them, I would not have known the real England any better than if I'd just read about it in a book. Most of the fellows over here don't bother to cultivate permanent friendships, and consequently never get to know the people or the place. A lot of fellows go to a different city every time they have a leave, and only judge it by the amount and price of liquor obtainable and the number of women they can pick up. They never get to know anything real.

I go to the Stamps' whenever I like, keep clothes etc. there... it is a home away from home— and as for a change of environment from the barracks, there is no place better.

You mentioned that I should get out with some people my own age— Mom, the Stamps are very young people for their age. And I am not trying to brag, although I suppose it sounds like it, but everyone takes me for 25 or 30 years old. One fellow said that and would not believe me when I showed him my paybook. I said, "It's because of my hair." He said, "No, you don't act like 22. Most guys of that age are bloody stupid."

The people I meet through the Stamps are worth knowing. They are well travelled and intelligent. If I lived the life of an ordinary soldier, I would be running around with third-rate tarts— and I certainly don't want to let myself get into that rut.

Don't think I am wasting away my life. I think the three things for my education that I can be thankful for are my home, the Stamps and Rose MacQueen. If I can't make a success of my life after all those blessings— and especially my home— then I only have myself to blame. But please don't think that I should forget the Stamps. They have been so darned good to me, that it would be an impossibility, and I could never do enought to repay them.

I got your tobacco for Christmas, Don, and posted you a letter. How about answering it? Anyway, once again, thanks very much.

Thanks for trying about the camera. I guess it is about the same over there as here. I hope this war won't last too much longer and I can be back home soon.

As for changing my dental unit, Mom, it is almost impossible. If I tried, God knows where I would end up; the higher-ups take a very poor view of requests for transfers. The boss is improving 100%, anyway. He stays in nearly every night and is a "model boy." Somebody told him why he had not got his promotion— and surprisingly enough, he took it to heart.

I am still keeping my hand in dentistry, and even do the odd job on the side. Our technician is a darned good head, and we have decided (unofficially) that he will work for me after the war. He does excellent work and is fast and interested. So that is one problem settled (more or less).

As for clothes, I am pretty well fixed— up till now, touch wood, we have had beautiful weather, for winter, anyway. They have the windows fixed and we are comfortable. Soon, though, we are going on a scheme— and no matter how many clothes one puts on, it is impossible to keep warm. But if that is the worst I have to put up with, I can't complain.

I am awfully glad you are feeling your old self again, Mother. It must have been an awful strain to go through all you have done in one jump. But I am also very glad that Trix could be so close to you and so good to you. I'll bet you'll miss her when she goes. The only thing we can do is hope that neither Trix nor Bob will have to be very far away from you.

Well, I better close now. Please don't worry about me being unhappy. For a time, nothing seemed to go right and I couldn't settle down. Now that Gray has straightened up and the sharp edges have worn off, I am feeling much better and happier. I am sorry I transferred my blues to your letters— but it is done now, and there is nothing one can do about it.

I intended to stop this long ago, so I'd better do it now. Do write soon and please don't worry. Keep smiling— as you say, it keeps up one's morale.

Lots of love,
Tom

February 18
Dear Mom,

We have been darned busy; any free moments I had, I rested. Your parcels were "gratefully received." Thanks a million.

Since Churchill's trip, the air has been tense with excitement over here. At last the war seems to be rolling. But then, every time it gets tense, nothing happens, so I don't know what to think.

Next week we are going out on a bit of a scheme and will have our mobile clinic. That is where I intend using your box of slab toffee. Chocolate is also very useful to have on schemes.

What do you think of the Russians? They sure are doing wonders. Every day they seem to get some big city or town. But according to today's papers, the Americans are taking quite a beating in Tunisia. I hope it will only be local, but it looks as though the First Army is going to have to withdraw.

Love,

Tom

February 25

Dear Mom,

Tonight I have a lot of "half news"— things that may or may not be.

But first of all I want to thank you— the tin of caramel slabs came in very handy on our scheme. You should have seen me using the straight razor★ for the first time! I almost had to stop shaving to laugh at the awkward positions I got myself into, but I am slowly getting the hang of it; it was a darn good idea of yours to send it.

You sure seem to be having your full share of winter weather. I don't want to make you jealous, but it has been almost like summer over here— an absolutely blue sky and strong sunshine.

I am sorry I have caused you so much worry. My blues seem to run in spells— I get along okay for a while, but then everything piles up to the point where I just have to blow off steam. Anyway— I heard last night from a fellow at H.Q. that we are to be separated and I am to be with a young new operator— but first, I am to take a course. That is only a rumour, and anything can happen at any moment.

Our scheme last weekend was my first serious one. It was more or less boring; we went through the motions. However, I learned quite a bit— and last night I wrote a six-page (foolscap) thesis on it which will go to the Colonel. He knows that I wrote it, so I hope it is a success.

I'm glad Don likes it where he is working. It is a darn good firm to work with and I think air transport will be the thing of the future. The workers in the aircraft industry over here are considered so important, they are treated even better than the Services.

Thanks so much for the subscription to *Readers Digest*. I received the first two copies last week, but did not know who they were from. So, once again, thanks a million. They are interesting, yet not too concentrated that you have to sit in perfect quietness to read them.

I am sorry to hear there is no entertainment at all over there now, but I guess it is the same everywhere. Over here there is absolutely nothing to do. In this village there is one small cinema with third-rate films. If anything good comes along, it means queueing for an hour. The dances are rotten— the village-hall type. But I guess we should consider ourselves lucky that we can still even have them.

What do you think of the war situation? According to tonight's news the Germans are in full retreat again.

Everyone here seems to be sitting on a powder keg which is ready to explode at any moment. But I guess I'd better shut up; they are tightening up on security.

Don't worry about me and know that I am thinking of you.

Love,

Tom

[*AUTHOR'S NOTE: When the razor arrived in a parcel, I must admit I wondered what my mother was thinking of. I had never used a straight razor, and Dad had never used one. It wasn't until a couple of letters later that she explained: she was worried because the Dental Corps worked under the aegis of the Red Cross— dental assistants were not allowed to carry arms. Mom thought— just in case— a razor might come in handy! I never, thank God, had to use it, but this shows what lengths a peace-loving woman will go to to protect her offspring.]

March 7

Dear Mom,

Please pardon me for not writing. We are out on a scheme and conditions are not the best.

We started last Sunday and are really getting around the country. Luckily, the weather has been beautiful except for a few days when it was cold and foggy.

The scheme has been most realistic, with planes, an army paper, iron rations and all— even tough living. I thought the other day, "If Mother could only see me now." I was almost frozen, filthy dirty, unshaven, hungry, and all that goes with it.

We are sleeping anywhere we stop, in hedges, ditches, leaves, straw stacks— anywhere— and are allowed only two blankets. So you know how comfortable we are.

Our food consists of bully beef, bacon, hard tack, jam, and tea. The men are divided into groups of 12 and one carton of food does each group for the day. There is enough, but it is monotonous. We are not allowed to buy food, bread, or anything else in any shop in England, and the shopkeepers have been warned not to sell us anything. We are supposed to experience actual operations and they are making conditions as near to that as possible.

Right now we are in the thick of battle and advancing. The town we have just captured is beautiful, and we are under cover on the village green. What more could one want on a lovely Sunday afternoon? But this morning we were in a cow pasture— and you know what that means underfoot. We arrived there about 3:45 in the morning after a six-hour trip. Went to "bed" and after a couple of hours' sleep had breakfast, shaved, and moved off again. On our trip this morning we were heavily "machine gunned." A beautiful sight in practice, but it would be as ugly if it were real. Planes swooped down on us and went right along the road about 15 feet overhead. The vibration of their motors shook the car— and that is no exaggeration.

As for dirt, I never knew I would be able to put up with so much. The worst morning was after a cold night; we spent the first half in the car and from 4:30 a.m. on in a haystack. Got up about 7:30 with no water and not enough time for food, drove for 3/4 of an hour and ended up in a Godforsaken gravel pit. Halfway through breakfast, we got the order to move again. Our mess tins were dirty from the night before— we had no water— the stove would not work, and everything went wrong. We moved off and took up positions in a farmyard. There was a very kind old lady there whose son was a gunner in Egypt; she gave us all the water we wanted. We heated some, and I stripped right down and had a bath in a foot-square tin box with about three inches of water. Not bad for the first part of March, eh?

I don't know how long we are going to stay out, but I hope it will not be too much longer. It is tougher than in actual operations as far as comforts go. We have to respect private property to some extent and cannot sleep in houses, etc. In actual war, we would take them all over. They are purposely making it tough for us now; later they will go out of their way to make it easier.

Well, Mom, I want to go and scrounge some water and wash my feet and change my socks. Later I am going to try and get some sleep as I didn't get much last night.

Hope you will excuse the pencil, but it is all I have at present.

Love,

Tom

March 10

Dear Don,

Happy Birthday, Don, and may you have many more. This letter will reach you late, but I hope you won't mind.

You sure are lucky not to be over here right now. We are out on a scheme and have been for a week and a half. It's a great way to see the country— cheaply, anyway— but God, the cold— and the food. We are allowed two blankets and a ground sheet and have to sleep anywhere we park. Last night we were on "Stand To," expecting an attack by about 50 tanks. Any of us who were allowed to sleep had to stay dressed, with boots right beside us along with our steel helmets. When I got up this morning, my helmet was frozen to the ground and my boots and gaiters covered with frost. The funny part is that I have not got the slightest bit of a cold.

Anyway, this is nearly over now... I hope— and we will be prepared for the real thing.

Today we have made two moves already and although it is now after five, we are starting out again, which means we will probably have to bed down in the blackout. But that is the way of the war— and believe me, it is no picnic.

While I am writing this, we are in convoy— miles and miles of military vehicles. We are making a retreat, so the roads are jammed.

The sky is full of planes covering our retreat. There must be 20 or 30 Mustangs zooming over the hedges, with some flying up higher. The tanks have broken through fences, over fields and even airports.

It is getting harder and harder to write in the jolting car, and I want to catch up on a bit of shut-eye.

As ever,
Tom

March 17

Dear Mom,

Three letters from you were there to welcome me back from the scheme— it sure was good after being away from "civilization" for so long.

Sounds like a darn good idea to make the house into a duplex, Mom. It will be less work and more cheery for you, besides the money it will bring. With that and the Moderwell house, you are really going into the real estate business, aren't you?

I'll write an ordinary letter soon.

Love,
Tom

March 25

Dear Mom,

Well, I received your second parcel just a week ago and there were the usual good things in it. The mice realized this, too; they ate their way through the cardboard and nibbled at the sugar, gobbled all the cheese in the macaroni box, chewed the spaghetti, and cleaned out one package of noodle soup. Other than that, though, everything was fine. Rationing sounds much stricter in Canada now; I don't know how you make your parcels so interesting and useful.

Love,
Tom

March 29

Dear Mom,

I had a 48-hour pass, and on Friday I went up to the Stamps'. Saturday, we all went over to a little village called Abinger, near Guildford. I wish you could have seen the beautiful old little hotel we stayed at. From the outside it was nothing much, but some parts of the inside took you back to the 1600s. One could imagine putting one's armour over the back of the chair and going to bed with a sword at one's side. The room was about eight feet by six, with bare white walls and very very old oak panelling and beams that were about a foot square. The windows were tiny, slightly crooked, and solid oak. Maybe this does not sound very beautiful, but it was the oldness and the simplicity and the atmosphere that made it so nice. The hallway ceiling was so low I almost had to duck my head, and I did have to duck to get into my room.

After dinner we had a few drinks and met one of the officers Clive has been training. He was an "Old Bill" type with the moustache and all, but had really been around. I think he is about the first Englishman I have met who knows the colonies and dominions better than he knows Europe. He has been to India, Burma, China, Japan, the States, Canada, and many smaller colonies in the east.

About eleven o'clock we went to bed and were up by five o'clock the following morning. Right after breakfast, Clive had to go out on training, so Moo and I took the bus to a little village called Shere about three miles away, and visited the "Silent Pool"— sounds dangerous, doesn't it? But it is all mixed up with the mythical stories of England. Some Lord is supposed to have drowned his chamber-maid— he was in love with her, or something to that effect— and the pool is supposed to be bottomless according to the story. But a few years back, the pool dried up, and lo and behold— it has a sandy bottom. This was apparently the butt of many jokes in England.

But the water is as clear as a bell and it gives the impression of great depth with the long weeds at the bottom of it. You can see huge trout floating lazily along.

The village of Shere is very very old. Way back, it was a place of importance— the centre of the iron industry— for coaches etc. All the "houses" were tiny cottages with solid oak doors and tiny, tiny windows, like dolls' houses.

Right in the centre of the village there is a big pond— I think it is part of a river, but it looks like a pond in a farmyard. The place is lousy with ducks which have been there forever and are more or less part of the village. They waddle up and down the roadway or cross it anywhere they please and nobody minds. When the ducks come to the roadway, they look both ways and then cross.

Sounds kind of stupid, doesn't it? But it is part of the quaintness of old England.

The people in the pub at the hotel were not very interesting— the usual pub crawlers Churchill referred to in his speech. They are a kind of standard organization over here. You get one bunch like it in every pub you go into.

But don't think a pub over here is the same as the beer parlours at home. Over here, everyone goes to the pub— from old ladies to young kids, and it is very seldom that anyone gets drunk. The average Englishman can make a pint of "bitters" last about four hours and never has more than a pint except on special occasions.

The thing I am trying to tell you is that the fact I go to pubs is not an indication that I'm a drunkard.

Back at Sleepy Hollow we had a light supper and I waited to hear Churchill speak. I only listened for half an hour as I had to catch a train.

It was a darn good speech, don't you think? About the most sensible plan for the future yet. After I left the Stamps', I took the bike to the nearest station and checked it there for Clive to pick up the following night as he came home from work. I spent the night in a "Y" canteen and was up at 5:30 the next morning to continue my journey, getting into camp at eight o'clock Monday morning. Ordinarily I would have left earlier, but if I had I would have missed all of Churchill's speech.

I guess I must have spring fever. I am so darned tired at nights that I can't think of anything but getting to bed.

Today the regiment went away on a shoot, so the dental unit had a very slack day. I made use of it to do my laundry, which had piled up considerably. Then I set up a complete upper denture for the first time, and although it took me quite a while, the technician said it was a darned good job. That is one of the things that if I get now I won't have to spend a lot of time on at school.

I am also studying textbooks so that it will be easier starting in.

Today, we heard the news that the Mareth line has been taken— darn good, eh what! I guess that means action for us shortly, but I think there is still quite a bit of fighting before the North African affair is entirely cleared up. Probably, though, the whole picture will have changed by the time you get this.

The tobacco and all the tinned stuff was lovely— and the caramel pudding was excellent. Frenchy and I had it here one night, cooking it in a mess tin with condensed milk and water.

I have to write the *War Diary* for last week, so I better close this for now and get the other finished. It has to go out tomorrow.

Good night, and keep fighting.

Love,
Tom

174 / TOM PATTERSON

April 9

Dear Mom,

Hello, again! I hope the house is finished and you can live a bit more comfortably. In your letter you sounded as if you were fed up with sawdust... I don't blame you.

Glad you decided to leave those bedrooms in the attic. That will make your part of the house almost as big as the part we used before. It will be awfully nice not to have to crowd when we come home. The financial end of it sounds good. I hope you can get tenants who will not be too much of a bother.

Your blood donor clinic seems to be going right along, Mom. I am glad it is a success and that you find the work so interesting.

From the look of things the Jerries are really going to concentrate on the St. Lawrence this summer. Quite a compliment to Canada, eh? Just shows how much the country has been sending out— as Anthony Eden just said— "An amazing war effort."

As you say, it would not be safe crossing now. I don't have too much worry about that, though, at least for myself.

Right above there are two squadrons of fighters returning from France— and they have their full complement of planes.

You are definitely right when you say that as long as we can laugh at silly things we will keep our sense of balance. I think it is the only way one can really get the best out of life.

Glad to hear you will be making more strawberry jam and hope to be able to taste it too. But don't think you have to send it over here. You need it just as well as we— in fact, in the winter you'll probably need it more.

How do you ever get on for tea, though? I often think you must almost die for a cup when you can only get an ounce a week.

Sorry I gave that impression about Canada, Mother. I really

didn't mean it that way; Canada is doing a magnificent job. In fact, we received a pamphlet from the Ministry of Information telling us about the transport question in general and it gave figures which proved that Canada was doing the biggest ship-building job per capita of any of the United Nations, including the States— and that is pretty good considering Canada started from nothing.

Last weekend I was at a Wings for Victory Week celebration in Headley with the Stamps. Everybody was all decked out in home-made costumes. It was a beautiful day and the bright sun on the bright uniforms was a powerful contrast to the deep sorrow underneath.

Honestly, Mom, some of these women deserve medals, they are so brave. Maybe most mothers are the same, but if they are then they all deserve medals. There was one woman there— about sixty I guess— selling War Savings Stamps to paste onto and cover a big swastika. Only a short time ago, she received word that one of her sons had been burned to death in the navy, and she has another son who is a prisoner of war in Italy. He tried to escape a little while ago but was caught, and is now in the worst Italian camp.

They also displayed the German flag that was hauled down from Tobruk the last time it was captured, by a nephew of another Headley family. It seemed that almost everyone at the celebration had sons in North Africa, the 8th Army, the navy, or who had just been killed.

Enough of that.

I still have some work to do before going to bed. I hope you have written Moo and Clive; they really enjoy getting your letters.

Sounds like a darn good idea, that trip over after the war. I sure would give an arm just to have you over here and be able to show you around along with the Stamps.

Love,

Tom

April 16

Dear Mom,

A very short note tonight, as I have a h——— of a lot of work to do and not much time to do it in.

Next week we are going on a scheme again; as we have no batman, I have to do all the work myself.

Once we get on scheme, I expect I will have spare time to catch up on my writing.

On Tuesday I received your nice long letter. I sure was glad to get it, Mom, and I know you did not mean that other stuff about the Stamps— you know— about my breaking with them.

It sounds like I am in quite a pleasant financial situation. I'm awfully glad, because it sure will come in handy. Thanks a lot.

Mom, be sure to take it easy when you start cleaning up the house; though by the time you get this you will likely have finished. All I can say is I hope it did not tire you out too much.

Moo and Clive got your letter this week. I was talking to Moo on the phone and she was very pleased with it. I hope your parcel to them gets over okay, too. It must be a hard job these days to make up parcels; it seems to be getting the same everywhere. Guess you were right about the limburger, but how I would have loved it. I certainly will appreciate the dill pickles.

Lots of love,
Tom

May 24

Dear Mother,

Well, today is a day of pretty big news— I hope. I sent you a telegram today asking you to make application at the Royal College of Dental

Surgeons for me, and also to get a testimonial as to my having obtained my Honour Matric.

I have been working on this for some time, but did not want to say anything about it in case it was another of those things. I am not counting on too much.

There is such a shortage of dentists that they are talking about sending the odd chair assistant to Canada for a sort of O.C.T.U. in dentistry; as soon as I heard about it, I applied. Nothing happened for a long time and then over the weekend, Grayson was talking to the Colonel and was told to have me get my testimonials etc.

There is a possibility of three chair assistants from this company going back, and the Colonel said my name headed the list. All I can do is hope.

We would remain in the army and be paid by the government, but I don't know at what rate. The course lasts approximately three years and we would graduate as Dental Officers. What they are going to do if the war is over, I don't know. Probably put us in the army of occupation, or somewhere like that.

I don't know when we would be due in Canada and won't believe even that I might be going until I get on the boat. But from what the Colonel says, they'd want us back for the fall term.

Mom, don't count on too much. It will just be that much harder if it does not come off, and you know how these things go.

I spent my nine-day leave with the Stamps. It was very quiet but very enjoyable. Nobody felt in a "holiday" mood, so we just went for bicycle rides, sunbathed etc. For the first two days I was as sick as a dog; too much sun, I guess, but I vomited the whole of one night. The next day I did not eat a thing and the second day I was back on my feet, though I felt pretty mothy. The rest of my leave was fine.

Moo had made an appointment to go to a blood donors' clinic, so I went with her and gave them 7/8 of a pint of my blood, too.

The rest of the time we cycled to various pubs for drinks and lunch or just lay in the garden.

Your hollyhock seeds are sprouting their third leaves. I hope they'll do even half as well as they do at home.

Yesterday Clive brought his Colonel, the Colonel's wife and their kid over for the day. They are very nice people and have invited us all back to their place. I don't know if I'll be able to go or not; things are getting more and more strict.

It was a darned good leave; almost like being home for a week.

The run comes out from H.Q. tomorrow, so maybe they will bring some mail.

Keep your fingers crossed for me.

Love,
Tom

July 16

Dear Mom,

Just a note to let you know I am still living.

Received your parcel this week, but I have not opened it yet; I am leaving it in the mail office until after I return from this course.

I'm sending a new address; I have been away from the Base Company so long, and there have been so many changes, that they don't remember me there any longer. This holds up the mail. If I move to a holding unit to go home, No. 2 Company will know where I am.

We are on this Driving Course at last— and it is a wonderful one. Guess who is on it with me?— none other than Freddie Church.

The two of us arrived here yesterday with all our equipment;

we were incredibly tired after hauling our stuff all over London. But we have good billets, good food, and lots of work. Our instructors are London Bus Company men who really know their stuff, as you can imagine. They are world renowned for their instructing. Today, our first day out, we drove all over Cheswick, Hammersmith, Acton, and out into the country— changing from second to third to fourth gear, then from fourth to second, then from second to third, and so on. We drive from 8:30 to 1:00, then have lunch in the Works Canteen, for which we are allowed one shilling. This buys a pretty good lunch— meat, potatoes, vegetable, dessert, and tea. We start again at 2:00 and go till 5:00. Then we parade back to our billets and have a good army supper.

Tomorrow we are going right into the heart of London. These guys don't waste any time. But this has to be one of the best and cheapest sightseeing trips possible. All one has to do is ask the instructor to go to a certain place and he will allow one to go. The final test— in two weeks time— takes place in the heart of London, in a three-ton lorry. We will just have to be able to drive by then— that or get killed. But these two instructors made me feel perfectly capable of driving before I even got in the truck. We had one young Frenchman today who had never driven before in his life; within half an hour he was going along in moderate traffic and making out fairly well.

Mom, it is getting dark, and my gear-shift arm is aching. I am lying in bed in my pyjamas, which is not the best place to write. Better get a little sleep— six o'clock comes early!

Love,

Tom

P.S. Please excuse the pencil and thin paper— it is all I could get.

August 17

Dear Mom,

Hello, again— I'm glad to hear that the Railway Unit arrived safely. They are a long way from me, so I doubt very much whether I shall be seeing any of them. But I hope I will.

You sure make me happy when you talk so definitely of seeing England. I do hope it will be in the not too distant future. And as you say, by the time you arrive I will know it pretty well.

There is nothing new on the dental course as yet.

Barney sure sounds pitiful. I have often wondered how he was, and wished he could live until I get back, but it doesn't sound as if he will. It sounds as if he is very faithful to you. I hate to mention it, but are you thinking of having him put down? It may be the kindest way. But then I guess you know what's best, so will shut up on the subject.

I do hope Bob can stay long enough to see the baby. It sure will be tough on him and Trix if he has to leave now.

On Sunday I heard Rawitz and Landauer playing the Warsaw Concerto. It was beautiful. I listen to these concerts every chance I get. The Stamps at last received a transformer for their radio. It has been over a year now since theirs burnt out, and in that time they have had to use a little portable radio with lousy tone. The new transformer has been on order so long that we had almost given up hope of ever receiving it. But now the symphony orchestras sound that much better.

No one knows anything definite about the war situation, and there is not much use in surmising. We sure are giving them hell from the air, though. God, it is thrilling to stand here and watch the bombers going out. Even to these people, who have seen so much of bombing and air forces— the pubs empty, people come out of their houses— and everybody wishes the pilots "Good luck," almost as if they were standing on the sidewalk beside them.

Bagdolio is going to be forced to throw in the sponge, I think; through his actions Italy has lost the chance for an honourable peace. If they had come clean when Mussolini first fell, they might have been treated as a bad boy. Feelings have changed.

The Russians seem to be pulling the hat trick again, and they seem annoyed that we have not done more. I think this may have been staged to fool Hitler. Old Winston knows what he is doing and why.

I'm enclosing some snaps which I hope you will like.

Love,
Tom

August 23

Dear Mom,

I thought I had better write to explain my telegram asking for £5.

I bought a $100 bond back in May. I would only have got a $50 one had I known we were still to be in England. Anyway, it has made quite a hole in my paybook. Then with all the changing around lately— Headquarters— London, back to H.Q.— leave, and now this new move, I have run pretty short again.

I hope you won't think I am becoming a gay dog or anything. It's circumstances, as they say.

Well, the unit that I am now attached to, is, I think, one of the best yet. The Sergeants' mess is darned good, the meals are excellent— and most of the fellows are very intelligent. By that I mean they are interested in things other than getting drunk and busting somebody's face in. They are the suicide squad of the army, too— being right up at the very front at all times. The Colonel is one of the best— a regular soldier and very strict on discipline, but also extremely sensible. When he says something he really means it, but he does not say stupid things and then end up having to carry them out, the way some of these Colonels do.

The clinic is very good. We have two wash basins, a work table, and a fairly large room for our clinic. The other two operators are in what was formerly the waiting room. In the back of the clinic are two showers, and we also have our own heating system. We are darn lucky. In fact, it is too nice— we shall probably move soon to some God-awful hole. It usually happens that way.

By the way, Sergeant Bricker— of Erie Street fame— is a member of the mess. We both went for about two days wondering where we had seen each other before, then finally had a chance to talk. I think he works on the M.T.

It sure would be nice to be home for Christmas, wouldn't it? God, what a present!! But it isn't much use in counting on it. No one knows how the army works.

Love,
Tom

October 11
Dear Mother,
Another week and still no mail! I do hope mine is getting back to you more frequently. If it is not, you will probably think I am lost in Naples or somewhere.

We have moved again, and for the first time are with an Ontario outfit— the R.H.L.I. from Hamilton. So you know what they are like! We are getting along pretty well.

We are in a woods again, sleeping in huts and working, for the time being, in the mobile clinic.

It sure is dead, too. But I guess nothing else can be expected.

There is still no news on the course. Gray was up to a dental meeting on Saturday and met Brigadier Lott, but he forgot to ask about the course. I think he was too interested in the fact that "Dearie" had had an interview with the Brigadier. I think she should consider herself damned lucky and let it drop at that. Gray has some kind of eczema, and that certainly won't do his dentistry any good.

But enough about him.

We get up at 6:45 in the morning, wash, shave, etc., breakfast, work from 8:15 to 5:00 and then sit around at night, usually in the N.A.A.F.I. canteen, and once or twice a week there are shows.

Last weekend I visited the Stamps. It felt good to get out in the garden and work. I have had one hell of a cold and have been getting a lot of stomach trouble (constipation) back again. But I think the gardening helped— that and a good night's sleep.

One thing I hate about sleeping in these huts: the blackout stays up all night and by morning it is as foul indoors as one can imagine. The floors are cement and get as dusty as hell. I hope that the next place will be better.

Last night, coming back to camp, I missed a train and had to go halfway around the south of England. I left at 7:00 and got back at 12:00— and it is only about 40 miles.

But that is usual wartime travel. And I had to walk the last three miles through a real old "pea souper." My cold doesn't seem any the worse for it, and it has seemed to start my stomach moving again, so today I feel pretty good.

Tonight, I am going to a YMCA show— *The Fleet's In* with Dorothy Lamour and William Holden.

October 12— 12:45. Hello again.

The run came out this morning and there was no mail for any of us. I suppose one of these days we'll get so much we'll have to take a day off to read it.

Meantime, keep smiling and hoping.

Lots of love,
Tom

December 3
Dear Mom,

I have to apologize for not writing sooner, but I have a good reason. I did not want to write in the middle of all that was happening until I found out that everything came off.

Yesterday I had one of the best days since being over here— I went to Parliament. And I think you will appreciate what a thrill that was— But, back to the beginning. Last weekend I met an M.P. while hitchhiking and he invited me to the House. I guess he did not figure I would take him up on it so soon. Anyway, I asked Gray on Monday morning if I could go— and he said he would have to ask the Colonel (because Gray won't take any responsibility). The Colonel said, "Certainly, as long as it is convenient for you." After he had gone, I asked Gray when I was going— to which he replied, "You'll go when I b—— well feel like letting you go." So I said, "Okay. I am asking for a transfer." So that was that. Then on Wednesday we moved, and after moving Gray told me I could have a pass for London on Tuesday— and then asked if I had changed my mind about the transfer. I fooled him and said no— and got the pass. So all day yesterday was spent in the House of Parliament listening to question time and to the debate. It is pretty hard to hear what they're saying— they don't cater to visitors by speaking up, but I heard Mr. Bevin, Mr. Atlee, and a few other bigshots, plus a lot of the private members.

Mr. Bevin introduced his scheme of a lottery to pick men for the coal mines, which caused a lot of heated argument. And don't think the English Parliament isn't democratic. One would think the cabinet ministers were a bunch of schoolboys being brought up on the carpet the way the private members fire questions at them.

I am keeping the "Orders of the Day" as a souvenir and hope to send it to you by air mail later on— but I won't send it during the Christmas rush.

I left Parliament about 4:30, went to a cinema, and saw Bette Davis and Paul Henreid in *Now Voyager*, which was an excellent show; at least I liked it a lot.

A very good day.

As for my move— I don't know when it will come, but I think it will be for the best, don't you? There is no use going into detail— you know as well as I what kind of guy Gray is. From the rumours, I am going to a pretty good fellow— another Major.

It seems as though you have not been getting very much mail, Mother. I'm sorry about that, but I have written every week except one for as long as I can remember. I hope you will have got them by now.

Phyl told me that I may be having a family reunion for Christmas— at least a partial one. I phoned Moo tonight and told her the good news— and Moo was thrilled— so if Bob is here in time we will have a huge Christmas party.

Everybody— Frenchy, another dental technician, and I are just starting to eat from our pooled resources: your chocolate and Oxo and someone else's shortbread. I'd better close; it is hard to eat, talk, and write at the same time.

But first I want to tell you about George Drew's letter.

I wrote Drew, congratulating him on his victory, etc., and today

I received a very nice reply from him. Of course, it was the usual thing, you know, but it was an answer to my letter, as he mentioned several points which I had brought up. So I will wait a little while and write him again.

I have some snaps now, but as Trix and Bob sent me the camera I am going to send some of them to them. I hope to have the snaps enlarged and when I do, I will send you some.

Lots of love,
Tom

December 21
Dear Phyl,

As you know by this time, the grand reunion has taken place. It really was good to see Bob. I don't think he has changed very much, except added a bit of weight.

I'm keeping my fingers crossed for Christmas. I have managed to get time off, but Bob seems to have moved and we cannot get in touch with him. He phoned the Stamps last Wednesday and that is the last we have heard. So I am hoping he has not been moved too far and will be able to get off this weekend.

How is Harry's cold? I hope it does not turn into flu as so many colds have been doing— over here at least.

How did Don make out on his medical? I do hope everything goes okay. I could just imagine him when Vera spoke of a deferment!

The china Mom got you sounds nice, and I wish I could contribute to it, too. But everything is utility over here, and unless one spends weeks looking around one can never find anything good. If I do see anything, I'll grab it up.

Sorry Harry has had to go so far away, but as you say he is still in Canada and that is something.

I was just listening to a radio program from the Italian front; two soldiers were saying that this was the last Christmas away from home. I hope they are right!

I'll be thinking of you at that party Trix has organized. Please let me know who plays the toilet paper and comb?

Love,

Tom

P.S. Moo sends her best

December 30

Dear Mom,

Today I was on the go from 5:00 a.m. to 7:30 p.m., with an hour and a quarter for dinner and 20 minutes for supper. There is a new dental page to be inserted in the paybooks and that is what I have been doing all day. Tonight my head is aching, my eyes are sore, my feet cold and my stomach upset. Otherwise I feel pretty good— and a good night's sleep will fix me up.

As you know by now, Bob and I spent Christmas together at the Stamps' and had a darned good time. I was really happy. Moo's mother and stepfather, Moo and Clive, and Bob and I made up the party and we all did okay. What pleased me most was to have one of the family here. And Bob, I think, felt as at home as I did. All the Stamps and their relatives liked Bob, too. We wrote an air-graph which I hope you have received by now.

I hope that in the not too distant future we may have a complete family party, with all of you meeting the Stamps and all of them meeting you. It will be fun, won't it, Mom?

But first of all, let's hope we have our reunion before very long!

Trix must be a wonderful girl, Mom. Everybody I have seen over here who knows her goes out of their way to say how nice she is. And most of the time people are too busy saying the opposite about other people to say kind things. I sure wish I could meet her personally. But I guess that day will come— and what a day.

We are very fortunate in being able to get along so well together. With Trix already "in" the family— and by "in" I mean it both ways— and Harry well on his way to the same position, well we are very fortunate— and that is putting it mildly.

You sure said it when you said "what a chance!" some people are taking in getting married.

This has seemed like old home week. I met Norm Carroll, whose mother used to cater at the Rotary luncheons. About five minutes later, I ran into Jim Gatschene. And funny thing— when he saw me, he looked absolutely amazed. He was reading a letter. He told me the next night that at the very moment I spoke to him, he was reading about Bob being on his way over here.

Being with Bob for Christmas and seeing these others, I almost imagined myself back in Stratford. Almost. There is a lot missing.

I'd better say good night; I'm nodding over the paper.

Love,

Tom

— 1944 —

January 4

Dear Mom,

To start off— the parcel I got was the one with Don's windbreaker in it— it is really a honey and I will write him tonight. The rest of the parcel was okay, too— in spite of the long time it took to get over here. That tomato soup is lovely. In fact, everything is. Last night we had some of your vanilla pudding and apple sauce. Captain Mackenzie received some Klem (powdered milk)— and between the two of us we did okay. I do like Phyl's cards, too.

Sorry Trix didn't get a letter from Bob, but don't be sore at him, Mom. I don't know why, but new men over here seem to have difficulty getting their mail through quickly. Whether it is because their mail clerks are new at the game or what, I don't know. But I do know that Bob is writing often. He asked me for some blue forms; they are very hard to get over here. So I gave him some and I know he thinks of Trix a lot and worries about how she is getting along. I don't think I have ever heard him express himself so fluently on any subject before. He really is in love, isn't he?

Bob phoned me on New Year's Day and seemed in pretty good shape. He is on a course, and some time this month will start another course very close to where I am— so we expect to see a bit more of one another.

190 / TOM PATTERSON

The braces you sent really came at the right time. The police braces are for ordinary everyday wear, and the others I save for leave.

How did you ever manage the sugar? It sure is good of you and I will be looking forward to it.

How is Don getting along in the Air Force? I don't wish him any bad luck, but I hope this thing is washed up before he has a chance to get over here.

Everything is going just the same for me. I sure am glad I left Grayson, and it makes me mad that I didn't do it sooner. The new officer, Captain Mackenzie, is really a swell guy. I couldn't have picked a better one. And it sure makes a difference.

Love,
Tom

January 4
Dear Don,
Received your Christmas present today and thanks a million. I am wearing the windbreaker right now; it could not have come at a better time. It is starting to get as cold as hell.

By the time you get this, you will probably be in Air Force blue. I sure hope you like it and that you get sent to a decent spot. Glad to hear that you passed your Medical A-1, too.

How is everything in Canada? Must seem kind of funny with no men around 132! I hope you are not too far away though, so that you can get home once in a while. The women would really appreciate it, I know.

Things are not much different over here; we are still sitting on our bums. But one of these days, I guess that will stop and a lot of fellows will wish they could get back.

The Air Force is giving the Huns a pounding. God, I don't know how they stand it. Guess there's not a hell of a lot they can do about it though. It's just a steady stream all day and all night with everything from fighters to four-engine jobs. Sometimes they make such a racket that you can't even hear yourself talk.

So far I have had two weekends with Bob, but in the middle of this month he is going on a course only a few miles from here— so we should be able to see a bit more of each other.

How about dropping a line when you get into the Air Force? Sure would like to hear from you.

> *As ever,*
> *Tom*

January 13
Dear Mom,

Received your letters tonight. I didn't write at the beginning of the week as there were no letters from you and I had a premonition that I would get some at the end of the week.

You don't know how nice it is to read your letters and know that you are happy and enjoying yourselves. It really does make a difference, Mom.

It was tough luck about your mince pies. I sure would have helped you get rid of them if I could have.

We had a pretty good Christmas dinner ourselves, considering— goose, Brussels sprouts (like very small cabbages) and other vegetables, Christmas pudding and mince pies. Bob brought a bottle of gin along and the Stamps had about three bottles plus some vermouth and of course, lots of beer. So we didn't do too badly.

I wish I could have been over at the Reids' with you when Wes got mouthy. I'd love to climb down his throat. The dirty b———.

How is Don getting on? I hope he never has to leave Canada. I guess it seems kind of funny with no men at all around the house. But maybe that condition won't last much longer.

Did Don get my letter? His coat is a beauty as you say, and fits perfectly. Several times already I have thanked my lucky stars that I have it. It really is warm, and hasn't the bulk of the greatcoats, which I hate wearing.

Phyl and Harry sure seem to be getting along. God how I wish this war could end and they could get married and all of us have a normal life again. This flying all over the place for moments of happiness is no good— even though those moments may be heaven.

It would be nice if Harry could be stationed in Toronto— or someplace near. I sure wish them luck.

You seem a happy family, though! I am so glad that Trix is living with you and is happy there. I think you're the grandest bunch in the world— and I mean that.

By this time you will have heard all about our Christmas party, but as you say, the Stamps are really nice. And, the same as you, I hope we can repay them when they come to Canada— and that, by the way, is more sure than ever now. They are really counting on it in every way. Oh yes, I gave you Clive's sock size but just in case— it is size 10 which I think means 10 inches. He has a very small foot. I know he would really appreciate your knitting for him. Moo has received your parcels and will be writing you soon.

We are just "carrying on" as usual over here. I hope to get a leave soon, and don't expect there will be anything to stop it. But I think I am just under the wire, if you know what I mean.

Hope to see Bob again soon. He is still in the same camp, but is moving some time this month, when I hope to see more of him.

Love,

Tom

February 15
Dear Mom,

How's everything? I finished my leave and I had a wonderful time. I met Bob for one weekend and you have probably heard all about it— Bob was writing to you while I was with him. Anyway, it was good to sit around and talk with him. The Saturday I got there, they had just come off an obstacle course, which from all accounts was something. Bob, as usual, came through with flying colours; the rest of the fellows were calling him "The Iron Man." It was really a tough go; everybody was so tired and sore that they could hardly move.

Bob met me on the bus on Saturday, and we went to the pub where we found a few of the other boys, and sat around there drinking beer until the last bus home— about 9:35.

The next morning we mooched around enjoying ourselves, even though it sounds a bit dull.

In the afternoon we went to the nearest city and saw a film, which wasn't too bad— but nothing exceptional. And after the show I continued on to the Stamps' and Bob went back to camp. He really has a swell bunch with him on the course. But Bob will have told you all about that.

Monday and Tuesday were also spent very quietly at the Stamps'. Wednesday, the four of us went up to London, starting off with a bit of shopping. And to show you the price of things, we bought three ordinary records which cost 3/3 each, making 9/9 in all. And added to that was a tax of 6/7, which made the three records about $3.50. But that is for luxuries, so no one can complain.

Then we had lunch at Hatchetts— a high class restaurant in Piccadilly. But the meals are just the same no matter where you go. The only difference is in price and atmosphere. After lunch we went to *Blithe Spirit*, the Noel Coward play. It was the story of a twice-married man who had a party to which he invited a spiritualist. And she called up the ghost of his first wife who couldn't be seen or heard by anyone but him. You can imagine the conversation when the ghost was in the room talking to him and he to her— with the second wife trying to get her bit in. It was really good. They are filming it in Hollywood now, I believe, so you may be seeing it soon.

Then we went out to Moo's mother's and spent the evening talking.

Thursday morning Clive and I went up to London early and did some shopping and then met Moo and her mother at the Café Royal for lunch. I had tripe for the first time. It is pretty good, I think. Have you ever had it?

In the afternoon we saw *Thousands Cheer*, which was okay, but nothing out of the ordinary, though the music in it was darned good.

The rest of the week we spent very quietly back at Sleepy Hollow.

Sunday we were going to go to the rugby game in London, but it was a bad day and travelling being so difficult, we decided to call it off.

Bob was up to see Jack Whyte, probably for the last time for a while. We met on the train going back to camp and so had a few hours together.

The mail has been very slow. Don't know what is going on, but I suppose one of these days it will come through with a bang.

Tonight I caught up with my laundry, which is all done now and drying.

Love,

Tom

February 17

Dear Phyl,

Your letter, which I received last Sunday night, sure was a pleasant return— or I should say a pleasant happening for an unhappy return. Those nine days of leave are lovely, but the more lovely they are, the worse that ninth night is— but you probably know all about that!

Tomorrow I'll post the minutes of the House of Commons session which I attended. Just thought I'd tell you so you will watch for them.

Well, I suppose by this time Harry is back east. I hope so— and that tomorrow's mail may bring me letters with good news— if you know what I mean!

Bob and I should have some pictures to send home pretty soon— but there are a few pictures left on the film, and we don't want to waste the films as they are valuable.

Friday— was interrupted last night...

As you say Phyl, it is queer how the boys, once home, want to get back here. It nearly always happens that way. They grouse because they cannot go back and then when they get there they want to be over here again.

I suppose they feel as if they are "in it" more over here— and it does get you that way.

So glad that Don is getting on okay. Gosh, we are lucky, aren't we— I mean the family— and especially the additions to it— Trix sounds wonderful— and Bob speaks the same about Harry— only hope I can keep up my end as well!

Have just been to see *Stormy Weather*— the all-coloured film, in the "Y" canteen. I thought it was pretty good— have you seen it?

While they were changing reels, I phoned Bob. He seems pretty tired— they were out all last night and most of today, I think.

I expect that as soon as he is over the course, he will spend a weekend at the Stamps'.

Give my best to Harry.

Love,
Tom

February 28
Dear Mom,

Last week I received 2,900 cigarettes— 300 from Don, 300 from Doc and Vera and 300 from Les and 1,000 from Trix— then on Friday, I got another 1,000 from Doc Smith, of all people! I also received the parcel with the shirt and tie in it; thanks, Mom. What a lovely parcel! And delicious tinned fruit salad!

Last weekend Bob and I went to a hotel in Brighton where the meals were 100% and the beds luxurious. The people in the hotel were a typical crowd— a retired Colonel and lots of other old people— one young couple— and an American lady— the "Madame Queen" type, who sat in the lounge with her bust sticking out, smoking a cigarette with a long holder and chewing gum. She told Bob she lived near Manitoba and then said in a further description that she was from Massachusetts. "Of course, that's nearer Halifax than it is to Manitoba, isn't it?" she said! Needless to say, she had lived here most of her life.

Bob is fine and this week sees the end of their course, which they are all thankful for!

I doubt if I've ever worked harder than we did last week, on the go about 16 hours out of every 24. But I don't mind; Captain Mackenzie is easy to work for.

I was offered an O.C.T.U. last week for the Artillery or Armoured Corps, but turned it down. I think it was the right thing to do. They couldn't make an officer out of me, in the military sense, in six weeks— especially now. I would hate to go into a unit of men who had been training for four years and be called a "stupid pipsqueak who knows f—— all." Accepting would have washed out all hopes in the Dental Corps, as far as after the war goes. I think it was the best thing, don't you? It would not have meant a trip home. Only Infantry O.C.T.U.s train in Canada now— at least those are the only soldiers sent from here.

Last week we had a few air raids; for a couple of nights it looked like old times. They weren't nearly as bad as they used to be, and our flak is really terrific now. In their immediate area, the flak is much more dangerous than bombs. But there has been nothing for the last four nights.

Love,
Tom

March 7

Dear Mom,

Everything in your package was appreciated more than I can say.

A few weeks ago we had the Corps Commanders' inspection— then the unit was inspected by General Montgomery, but we were not seen on that one— and this week we are having someone else, bigger than ever. I don't know whether we will be involved, though I hope so. In any case, we have to get ready.

I don't think weariness is having any great effect on most people, Mom, but Moo is all alone most of the day and about three nights a week— and as she lives in the country with no one else around, she gets pretty fed up. Not only that, she doesn't like the cold damp of the winter and it usually manages to get her down, but she picks up as soon as she is with friends. Honestly, there is hardly anything to do over here in winter time. The buses stop early— and everything else, for that matter. There is hardly any use going out after work.

I haven't seen Bob for 10 days— he has gone back to the Reinforcement Unit. I'll try to contact him.

Captain Mackenzie is a swell guy to work for. There is some talk of chair assistants being rotated now— a different operator every three months or so. Last night Mackenzie told me he would appreciate it if I asked the Colonel if I could stay here, that is, if I want to. So I guess I must be doing okay.

Love,
Tom

March 12
Dear Mom,
Bob and I spent last weekend with the Stamps. It was very quiet— on Sunday afternoon, we wandered up to the camp near there and met Sol Gerofsky and Arn. Schlauss and had a couple of beers with them. The Stamps wanted us to bring these fellows to tea, but they were in old clothes and unshaved and so could not come.

Tonight there is a Canadian concert party in camp and they are supposed to have a pretty good show. Some of the C.W.A.C.s in it were in for dental treatment this afternoon and one of them came from Forest Hill and knew the Aikenheads and Bob Whyte. Seemed kind of funny talking to Canadian girls who knew friends back home.

Bob received the news about the baby last week and was very relieved for Trix's sake. Don't worry too much about him not writing. He has been pretty worried about Trix; that is all he could think of. Don't think he meant anything by not writing, Mom. He felt pretty ashamed about it, really. Now that things will run smoothly for Trix, I think he will be much better.

Love,

Tom

March 21
Dear Mom,

Your last package had had quite a journey. The candy and peanuts were all over the box and stuck to everything. However, they did not lose any of their taste, so no complaints! I am saving the tinned chicken for the weekend, but gosh it looks nice!

I am not at H.Q. It is not bad, but I will be glad when I get back. Captain Mackenzie is on leave and that is the reason I am here.

Sunday I got a pass to the rugby game in which Bob played. They were pretty good, but the Canadian team lacked practice and was beaten 18-0. The Yanks had been playing together since last November, so it is nothing to be ashamed of. I talked to Bob for a couple of minutes after the game, but over a 20-foot barrier; we couldn't say much. I haven't heard from Bob since.

The air forces are doing a wonderful job— every day they seem to be sending more and more planes over. According to today's paper, Hungary is finished as a German ally. A few more like that, and the war will be finished much sooner. But there is no use counting on it.

Also, it was announced this morning that the whole south coast of England is banned to visitors. It is the first time such a large area has been put under the ban. But as far as I am concerned, it does not mean much, if you know what I mean.

All day we work on army stuff, and all evening on our own

stuff— I am going to make a brooch or pin and send it in a letter as soon as I get it finished.

How is Trix now? I was very sorry to hear about the baby, but as you say, it is for the best. I wrote Trix but am afraid I bungled the letter. Please explain to her, will you?

Love,
Tom

March 31
Dear Mom,

The jelly beans and chocolate you sent are already gone. The tinned foods have gone into our "reserve stock." Captain Mackenzie and I have a box to which we make donations from every parcel; the box will accompany us on schemes etc. Right now we are sitting pretty.

Sunday morning we are having a cocktail party. At noon today, I found out how I could get a couple of bottles of gin and one of sherry. I phoned Moo, and Sunday is the result. Sure hope nothing turns up to stop it.

I have not heard from Bob for a couple of weeks, but he will have been pretty busy. I think he has moved and is now quite a way from us. I should hear something more definite soon.

It maybe sounds queer when I say there is little to report when so much seems to be about to happen, but we are all in the dark.

I can say that we are making our second front effort now. Captain Mackenzie tells me that the least we can do is try and get the boys fixed up before they go. We are working hard. Every night this week it was 12:00 or 1:00 in the morning before we got to bed— and that is a son of a gun when one has to stay in one small room all day and then all evening. However, it is worth it; I'm not kicking.

By the way, I want to thank you for *Public Opinion, Canada at*

War and the *Beacon-Herald* which you sent in the parcel. So far I have only read *Public Opinion*— which I think is damned good. They are really opening up the C.C.F. and telling people what they are, don't you think? It is a darn good paper for a political organization and from the sounds of things the Progressive Conservatives figure to win the coming election. I hope so.

Love,
Tom

April 10
Dear Mom,

I felt pretty tough and tired all last week and it culminated in a touch of the flu on Friday night. So I went to bed and am now in the unit sick bay. It is nothing serious, so don't worry. I expect to be out tomorrow.

I'll be able to go to a party at the Stamps' Easter weekend— this is the first time since I have been in the army that I have been confined to bed! They went ahead, and their party came off all right; last night I got up to wash, had supper, phoned Moo and went back to bed.

They saved a bottle so we are going to build up on that and have another.

Heard from Bob last week. He is in the same camp where I was for nearly two years. It is a good camp, but the people there are not the same as they used to be. From what I hear there is a large number of lead swingers. But he may have a good bunch. I hope so.

Tuesday— I fell asleep after dinner yesterday. And this afternoon the M.O. let me get up. I've been wandering around getting my "legs" back and feel 100%.

Have just received a call from Bob. You probably have heard his news so I won't go into it here. I hope to see him soon.

How is Don getting on in the Air Force? I hope he will be okay.

Glad to hear that the business end of the factory is so good. I guess it will take a load off your mind too, eh? Congratulations and keep up the good work!

There is so much to say— but one has to guard every word.

Love,
Tom

April 21

Dear Mom,

Last weekend I saw Bob for a few hours. I missed the last train on Saturday night, so had to stay till Sunday morning, and Bob and I walked to the station together. I don't think I have ever been so worried about getting back to camp, but I made it; I was late, but it was okay.

Bob and I are posted quite a distance from each other, so I probably will not be seeing him for some time. It was good while it lasted!

As for me, I have gone back just about ten years, to camping at Kitchigami— only we went *there* for a holiday! All in all, though, it is pretty good. The food is not bad, and the fresh air has made me so damned sleepy that I can just roll over anywhere and snooze.

And when I think that had I not changed operators, I would have had to live this life with Gray— God, it makes me happy to be away from him.

I can't say anything about what a good guy Captain Mackenzie is, because, you see, he has to read this.

(Don't eat that, Elmer!)

(That last sentence is strictly for the censor.)

But we have got a heck of a good driver-orderly with us now— a lot of fun and a hell of a good worker, so really we are just one happy family— or something!

Oh, yes— I tried to send you flowers on Mothers' Day, but I can't make arrangements from here. You will just have to take my word that I am thinking of you and hoping that by this time next year I can go down to Jeffries' myself and order the flowers.

Look after yourself.

> *Love,*
> *Tom*

April 30
Dear Mom,

Sorry to hear that you are feeling kind of fed up. I guess there is not much one can do. Everyone seems to get that way every so often. So cheer up— this mess might be over soon and then we can all go back to living our own lives and being our own bosses, instead of being dictated to by the bigshots in Ottawa.

It sure is good to know that the estate has finally been settled.

Yesterday I went into a famous town and wandered around in the afternoon and then had dinner at quite a nice hotel— a good meal— roast chicken, potatoes, and cabbage. Maybe that doesn't sound very exciting, but it was good.

The place was so crowded with troops that one could hardly move on the streets; I had a 24-hour pass but did not use it. That is the first time this has ever happened to me!

Have not seen Bob for some time, but I expect he is quite busy.

> *Love,*
> *Tom*

May 3

Dear Phyl,

As I am writing this, there is quite a war-like scene going on. In the valley below us, flamethrowers are belching back and forth. On the hill overlooking them are some tanks, and overhead the planes are roaring— and besides all that the wind is blowing like hell.

Last night, a Spitfire cracked up not far from the camp. It had returned from France pretty shot up. The pilot, a Pole, bailed out and the plane landed in a field, barely missing a farmer's cottage. Luckily, no one was hurt.

I have seen a famous cathedral and attended a service there. Nearly every night Captain Mackenzie and I and sometimes one or two of the boys go for a walk in the beautiful country around here. We usually end up at the N.A.A.F.I. and have a beer and then head back to the clinic for something to eat. The last couple of nights we had mushroom soup— and it was really good. We have also been very lucky in finding a dairy that supplies us with the odd egg. All in all we do quite well for ourselves.

Have not seen Bob for some time, but I got a letter from him on Monday, and he sounded quite happy.

The only thing one can do is live day to day without thinking of tomorrow. Otherwise, one would go completely nuts— and I do mean nuts.

The air, good food, and exercise have combined to make me feel better than I have for a long time.

I'd better close now and allow room for the censor to sign this. Give my best to Harry.

Love,

Tom

May 16

Dear Mom,

I haven't seen Bob for over a month, but in his letter to me he was in good spirits and satisfied.

Glad that Phyl is being successful on the radio. Maybe she will be a star when I get back.

Sorry that Moo Stamp seemed so casual about the parcel, Mom, but don't think she felt that way. Every time she hears mention of a parcel going to her, she's thrilled. Maybe she didn't feel well. And you are right about fear of the censor. Moo's stepfather is a censor; she knows what they look for and is more cautious than the ordinary person. But she appreciates your parcels very much and thinks you are kind and generous to send them. About the stockings— you told me you were sending them, and they should have arrived— but they haven't. I have not had a chance to see the Stamps for over a month; phoning is pretty expensive and it's hard to get through. So I don't know exactly what is going on.

Thanks for the $300 bond you got me— it is by far the best investment to make. I also bought a $50 bond over here. It will be sent to you to look after, the same as the $100 one was.

Last Saturday I was in a famous town with a huge old castle overlooking it. The castle has been taken over by troops, and we were allowed in. From the top you can really see a long way, though it was not a very clear day.

After leaving the castle, I came down into the market square where there was a stall selling fresh crabs, so I had some. It was really funny, Mom— a whole lot of soldiers standing around this stall with the old fish woman going from one to the other showing them how to eat the crab.

The poem that Moo sent Phyl reminds me very much of this town— especially the title.

You know, if I had the same thing to do over again, I wouldn't change it. Being over here, even under these conditions, has broadened me more than anything else could have. So I am not kicking, but I wish it would end and that we could all get back to normal.

Love,
Tom

May 25

Dear Mom,

Some nights we pool all our food "resources" and really have a good meal— besides the fun of cooking it! So thanks for the parcel and very much for getting the bond. I should be pretty well off now, shouldn't I? Could you let me know exactly how much I have in bonds, and also check my insurance? I am paying for one policy, but Dad was paying for another— and I don't know what's become of that. Mac Hall told me it was okay but that was quite a while ago.

Sorry that Moo seemed so depressed in her letter. God, Mom, it is rough on her.

Friday— It was pretty late when we finished last night, so I left this till this morning. We had chicken on toast, vegetable soup, and coffee. Mom, that mushroom soup is more than appreciated.

But here comes the run from H.Q.—

Back again— thanks for the tube of shaving cream. It is impossible to get it any other way than in jars over here, and they are so damn hard to carry. Thanks for the paté de fois. It is delicious. Will you thank Don again for the windbreaker? It has been in almost 24-hour service. I wear it ordinarily with my gown and at night use it to cover my feet in bed, having my greatcoat for the top half. It looks very nice and is always being noticed and coveted.

Have you heard from Bob? By the sound of things he will have a bit of excitement down there. We heard that the 5th Army has linked up with the Anzio beachhead. I don't know whether this is true or not.

Did I tell you that I wrote to *Public Opinion* about their paper? Anyway, I did. For the last couple of weeks I have been reading more than enough politics. First of all— the two *Public Opinions* you sent, then I found a Penguin *Hansard* which started just before the war and came as far as Churchill's "blood, tears, and sweat" speech. I really enjoyed it— more so since I have actually been in the Commons and could picture the whole thing.

I have been writing this disjointed letter at odd moments through the whole morning, so... keep smiling.

Love,
Tom

May 31

Dear Mom,

Last night I got an air-mail note from Bob, and also received word from Moo Stamp that she'd received your parcel with the two pair of stockings. She was delighted. Clive got the knitted socks from Phyl. Expect a letter any time— although it probably won't go over as fast as this one does. They told me to thank you.

From the clippings you have sent, the Pattersons sure seem to be in the running in Stratford. I am glad you have something to keep you busy, especially in these times.

The marrying bug seems to have visited town lately, hasn't it? Almost every letter I get tells me about another marriage!

Gosh, Mom, I am disgusted with Morley B. Of all the weak-livered s———, he is the worst. He is out for his crown and I think if he could lick the Colonel's boots, he would. But enough bitching.

Bob seems to find his new home interesting, but very, very filthy.

It must have been quite a shock when you answered the phone and heard Harry's voice telling you he is back east. I'm glad Phyl and Harry can be together for a while. When do you think they will "take the aisle"? Or is that an embarrassing question?

Love,
Tom

June 9

Dear Mom,

Received your dill pickles today— do they ever look good! At the moment they are sitting on the trunk beside me— and all day long I have been tempted to open them. But I am going to save them for Sunday; I hope to have a bit of a celebration for June 11.

I haven't been quite so strong-willed with the nuts though, having just finished the last one. So thanks a lot.

When I thanked you for the last parcel, I had not noticed the type of toilet paper you sent— I really got a laugh out of those "proverbs."

Well, the thing we have been waiting for, for the last four years, has finally come off...

And we have been busy— last Sunday we worked from 7:00 in the morning until 9:00 at night, outdoor work, too. I did not get a good sleep until Monday night. But Tuesday— "D-Day"— I felt fine.

Last night we had a bit of a "do" in the clinic, one of those spontaneous things. Everybody had a good time— the only trouble was that there was nowhere to go for dancing and music. Nevertheless, we can't have everything.

Have you heard from the Stamps? If not, there is a letter on its way. I phoned them tonight and they both send their best.

I received a letter from the Progressive Conservative Party H.Q. It was not the usual stereotyped sort of thing, and arrived by return mail— not bad, do you think?

Bob has written only once since he left...

It is four years last Sunday when I left home. The boys in France seem to be really going places, and I hope it's all finished soon— not only for my own sake— but for that of the whole world.

Mom, as a special war effort, you could try and get as many people as you can to write the boys over here. I don't mean that for myself but for everybody. You have no idea how much a letter from home means. And now that things are getting tougher, letters are even more important. Just to show you how much the authorities think of them— the first mail has already been landed in France— and that is something when one considers how much other seemingly more important stuff has to be handled.

As you will see by the picture I am very healthy and happy. What do you think? (Barring the hair, of course.) I have got a bit more than shows in the picture though!

Love,

Tom

June 13

Dear Mom,

My birthday has come and gone— and I wished that annual wish— that it would be the last one spent away from home.

I did have a pretty good day just the same. On Saturday at midnight, Captain Mackenzie and Captain Mason— another dental officer stationed close by— presented me with a bottle of gin— which was extremely good of them. Sunday morning I had a bath— my birthday present to myself— in Captain Mac's canvas tub— the same one in the picture I sent. Sunday afternoon we went to the show in town and saw Judy Canova and the Invasion pictures. Then we came back to camp— made our own meal— Captain Mac's meatballs, your chicken and Captain Mac's peaches— and drank the bottle of gin and ate your cucumbers. So as you can see— we did all right.

Now we are back to normal— sleeping, eating, and lots of work.

The paper this morning said that Churchill and Eisenhower both landed on the beaches yesterday, after the successful invasion. Things must be going pretty well. No casualties have been announced; they seem to be much lighter than was suspected at first.

Last night it was quite noisy here— although nothing dangerous in our immediate vicinity. I heard one bang— then went back to sleep and didn't hear another thing until about 7:30 this morning. Today things have been rather quiet but our boys are starting out again tonight.

While I am writing, the boss is enjoying a bath on the clinic floor. He really looks "comfortable." But a hot bath is a hot bath— and not to be laughed at— but I wish I had a camera!

Love,

Tom

211 / THEY NEVER RATIONED COURAGE

June 23

Dear Mom,

Thanks for the birthday greetings— and don't worry about the money. At present, I have no need of it; there is hardly anywhere to spend it and my pay takes care of everything. Next leave, though— if and when— it would be really appreciated.

No, Mother, I'm afraid I was not in the fortunate position of having anything to do with the invasion. No, not even by making a wounded soldier comfortable. But there were quite a few others in the same position, so I musn't complain.

I imagine you are getting a detailed description of the fighting. But the closer one is to the battlefield the less one knows— or at least that is the way it seems to go. According to tonight's news, Cherbourg is expected to fall at any moment. It is being heavily shelled by Army, Navy, and Air Force. And that is usually a sign that the end of fighting in a place is very close.

You will have heard that we are being attacked here by the Robot Plane. I don't know what Jerry is trying to do, because as military weapons the Robots are an absolute flop— and, as far as morale goes, there are one or two little things— like our invasions— going on, which more than offset the flying bomb. It is, all round, a complete flaperoo as a secret weapon.

Love,
Tom

July 8

Dear Mom,

I have once again changed my address, and I am now "somewhere in France." But do not worry. It took four years of waiting to get here, so here's hoping it will not take that long to get back home to

212 / TOM PATTERSON

Canada. Anyway, we have been in such a muddle moving from here to there, and from there to somewhere else, that I haven't been able to write.

How is everything at home? The mail was very slow in getting through, but in the last two days it has changed completely and letters from Canada are reaching here in eight days. Mine will be slower because I am attached out.

Conditions here are much better than I expected. Comparatively little damage has been done, considering the size of the operation.

We are eating well, but the drinking situation is bad. The water is putrid and the only way we have found to take the taste away is with the Oxo cubes which I have been saving from your parcels. Even tea doesn't take the taste away.

There are three of us together— Captain Mackenzie, Sergeant Joe Poole and I. Phyl met Joe at Union Station in Toronto when we were on our way to Halifax. Joe says to give his best to Phyl and ask her if she has that bottle of beer she promised on ice for him, because he can almost taste it.

I have not seen any Frenchmen up close, so I cannot say what they are like. If one listens to the rumours, they are everything from ultra-fifth-columnists to ultra-United Nationists.

In due time, I will see for myself.

Our trip over was glorious as a pleasure cruise— only a bit crowded. I managed to sunburn my face; it was really sore, but it's okay now.

When we came in to land, we passed a barge with a loudspeaker on it and were greeted with, "Good evening, 'Joe,'" (Joe stands in for the name of our ship), as if we were entering a dance hall or formal party.

Have you heard from Bob? I wrote him some time ago, but don't know whether he got the letter or not.

Mom, be sure not to worry about me; I can get along okay and look after myself.

Love,
Tom

July 14
Dear Mom,

We are not very busy doing dentistry, but have done enough work to make our journey worthwhile. We only do emergency work— extractions, treating trench mouth, etc. When things are slack here, I try to give a hand to the medical boys if they are busy. For the first few days nearly everyone was going "stir crazy," but things have changed; war is not glorious— not even a little bit. It seemed easy, sitting back comfortably, reading the deeds of heroic men— but when one sees those men in all the filth and grime and pain, one realizes that it is guts and raw bravery, and not much glory.

There is no need to worry about me. I am in a safe position and am pleased with the way I have reacted.

But let's get away from war and talk about something pleasant. That strawberry jam you mentioned makes my mouth water. Our food is not the most delicate— although we have plenty. I sure am looking forward to the jam.

Also thanks for the £5. Even in France I can have it changed or arrange to have it "banked" in my paybook. I think I will do that; so far I have not spent a sou here. But it will really come in handy if and when we get leaves back to England.

Please write soon. Letters are really valuable here. And if you don't hear from me for a while, which is unlikely, don't worry. No news is good news in this case. If anything does happen, which is also most unlikely, you will be notified within 24 hours— even for a minor injury not connected with the war at all.

Love,

Tom

July 23
Dear Mom,

I'm glad those snaps of Bob and I turned out okay. We did look like two billiard balls, but then our hair (what there is of it) is definitely not photogenic.

It seems there is a bit of trouble in Berlin. I only hope some new "Joe" doesn't come along and take over the German government, fake peace and then prepare for another war.

The Canadian people are very patriotic, aren't they? It is wonderful the way some people, especially those rich old ladies, buckle down and help out. Of course, some are very selfish, but I think the majority of people are not.

I certainly would appreciate that pamphlet about post-war rehabilitation. I haven't seen anything about it over here— and especially in France, such things are hard to obtain.

The "not anywhere" where we are is quite historic (as all of France is!) but we are not allowed to see any of it. The few people we have met seem genuinely friendly. They have suffered so much since "D-Day," through the fighting, that they are more or less stunned. They have lost everything they owned and must wonder if it was worthwhile being liberated. The Germans apparently acted very well in this part of the country. Just the same, as a whole, the French are glad we are here.

Our living conditions are not the best, although we cannot

complain, under the circumstances. I am covered with spots—
almost everyone is the same. I only hope it is not lice (or as they are
called, Mexican jumping fleas). Whatever they are, they are miserable. The food is very very monotonous, but we can expect nothing
better for a while. We do get candy and a chocolate bar daily, but I
do not eat mine. They are a definite asset in a tight spot or to use as
an introduction to the French people.

Love,
Tom

September 16
Dear Mom,
If the war keeps moving at this speed, I won't mind the lack of mail
nearly so much.

Glad you have received the official documents, and that the estate
is all cleaned up. As you say, if we all keep our heads (which I am
quite sure we will do), everything will stay satisfactory.

My letter to the Gatschenes about the death of their son arrived
at the right time. It would've been awful if it had got there before
the official news. I hate to think of it.

I have not seen the grave, but I've been told that when it was
about two weeks old it was completely covered, by the French
people, with all kinds of flowers. I wouldn't tell Ma and Pa that he
received last rites, for fear they get a letter from the R.C. padre saying
otherwise, which is possible. I haven't had a chance to speak to the
man in charge of the burial party to find out any of the details.

I'm glad to hear you wrote to the Stamps and are sending them
a parcel. I would hate to have them think that now I am out of
England, we are forgetting all about them.

Your dinner party sounds quite an affair (besides quite a meal).

I only wish I could have added to your supplies; the other day, we had two bottles of champagne which were taken, with a lot of other liquor and wines, and men, from a German fortress. That would have gone all right, don't you think?

Our life here is really something. Innumerable kids hang around the camp from 7:00 a.m. to 11:00 at night. They have attached themselves to individuals, so that everyone has a shadow who acts almost as a batman. If we want eggs, tomatoes, or fruit, we send our shadows out and in no time they are back with our desires. Tonight I am on duty, so my shadow brought me two bottles of beer. We are eating almost like kings— the other night we had fried sausage, potatoes, green peas, corn on the cob, apple pie and ice cream. Pretty good for an army supper.

Practically every night I visit a small café where I have met a nice family. We sit and drink beer, the national drink, and then go to their home where we have eggs, tomatoes, and potatoes. Last night we had eels. It almost made me sick to watch them being prepared. With the usual Continental hardness, they cleaned them before killing them. I had to eat them but they tasted quite nice.

I am learning some Flemish and teaching English— with French as a go-between, which is funny, considering my French.

Captain Mackenzie is back, which makes me very happy. So far we have not been sent out on detachment and are doing practically nothing. But the rest is really worthwhile, especially if we can live a bit of civilized life. There are many nice and happy people.

Glad to hear that you went to church on the National Day of Prayer, but it's better to pray every day. I may sound a bit old fashioned, but I don't think so. Living over here has taught me that people are more religious than they let on in ordinary times. Prayer is really something. Don't let anyone tell you differently.

Phyl and Harry seem to be having quite a tough time. I do hope they can get together soon and that the Air Force will not disturb their plans any more.

Mom, I'm afraid I won't come home quite the same as I left. I'm much broader minded, I hope, and more understanding. But thanks for the thought.

As they say over here, "Guten Nacht," and keep happy.

Love,

Tom

September 21

Dear Sirs,

Once again I have the pleasure of thanking you for your gift of cigarettes— a gift which is much more valuable than even money.

Cigarettes have a double value over here. Besides giving the boys pleasure and relaxation, which is close to a necessity, they help break down the language barrier, which, when we are moving so fast, is hard to accomplish.

It's as if Jerry commandeered the whole tobacco crop of Europe. Consequently the civil population goes for cigarettes as much as food.

I hope that it will not be long now before you can relax in your duties and in fact give them up all together.

I want to thank you most sincerely for the way you are looking after us; all the boys from Stratford feel exactly the same. It is really something to know that after five long years, the people at home still remember and think of us.

Once again— thanks, and I hope it will not be too long before I can thank you in person.

Sincerely,

H. Patterson

October 16

Dear Mom,

Thank you for the names of your friends in the Dutch army. I will try to make some connection with them in Holland— if we go there.

And thanks for sending stuff to the Stamps. In her last letter, Moo said she had heard from you and written you. I do hope your parcels arrive in time for Christmas.

Your news about air travel to and from Europe is encouraging— and we absolutely must visit here after the war. There are so many things to see— and learn— in this world, that I am afraid I won't want to settle down for quite a while yet. A day hardly passes that I don't think of what I would be doing if I was visiting these places as a civilian. Of course, there are immense advantages in being in the army; it is easy to meet people, and travel is cheaper. But one is also restricted and cannot see the most interesting things— so, as you say— here's hoping!

Mother, do you think there is any possibility of me getting a job with, say, the *Beacon* and a couple of the other small papers, so that when I return here, I could write perhaps one story a week for them, and so help pay for the trip? What do you think of the idea? If it is okay with you, how about mentioning it to Tom Dolan or someone like that, and seeing what they think?

By the time you get this, it may be too late— but I would be very glad if you would get me a $300 bond in this loan. Have you received the $50 one that I sent in the last loan?

By the time the 8th Campaign begins I should be home, or at least on my way— so I think I'd better stop buying bonds now, and save the ready cash, which will be very necessary on demobbing, I think.

As you suggested— I am doing lots of "speakin'." It is difficult sometimes because of the language barrier, but I am getting along. Besides understanding many things better than I did, my French is improving— but it has a hell of a long way to go yet. I am afraid Miss Stuart would be horrified if she could hear me.

Love,

Tom

November 17

Dear Mom,

Thanks so much for the package. I am saving most of the corn, chicken etc. towards a big meal later on— I hope when I can meet some interesting people.

Thanks for the pipe tobacco you nearly always send. It comes in very handy, especially at night— and it is an extremely good brand. Is it popular in Canada now? I have never heard of it before.

Since I got back from my pass, we have been going fast and steady, and it has been cold at night.

We are in Holland, and so far it is a pretty miserable place. My conversation with one of the locals describes the weather perfectly. It was pouring rain, so I said, "Much water." He said "Vader vader?— das Hollandt." Even when there is no rain, it is still wet. And now it is cold also. Still, I must not complain; there are many other men who live under much worse conditions than I.

We have not seen anything but the real "backwoods" of the country. Although it is dull, some of the scenes are very picturesque. There are windmills everywhere, which is unique. Added to that are the fat waddling old women, some with bonnets, and the old-fashioned men with pipes and hands in pockets, all wearing wooden shoes— it is a picture I thought one could not have seen for the last 100 years. However, it is as true today as it ever was.

We are billeted with a Dutch family. You would have laughed last night, if you had seen us. Four of us were invited to the dining room to sit around the fire with the family. The children, ranging from 24 to 10, are all learning English, and the conversation was funny. The old man sat there with his pipe in his mouth and his hat on the side of his head, not saying very much— and what he did say was in Dutch. The mother sat in the corner working the wool in preparation for weaving— while all the kids tried to talk to us. All of this was done under the light of one lamp in the middle of the table.

The people are kindness itself. They want to do everything for us, including washing. But the language barrier is no help. In France, enough boys could speak French, and in Belgium nearly every second person spoke English— and those who didn't could always get by with French. But hardly any of us can speak Dutch— and very few Dutchmen can speak English. Nevertheless, we get along.

In spite of the weather, the last two days have made me very happy. Yesterday, I received letters from Bob, and Moo Stamp— and today we heard *rumours* that those with five years' continuous overseas service were to get 30 days' leave in Canada; and service in France counts double. Unfortunately, I am one-and-a-half months short, so will not be going in the first bunch, which is supposed to arrive for Christmas.

If nothing happens I should be able to leave about December 15, but you know how the army goes, and I am not going to let myself in for a letdown, like last time, by counting on it too much. However, I will keep you posted.

Bob seemed very well, although, like all of us, he was wishing this bloody mess was over.

Sorry to hear about Trix's mother and hope by now she is okay.

Trix has had too much tragedy in the last few years. I will write her as soon as I can.

I don't think Don could have sent me a better Christmas present than he did last year. Its usefulness is beyond words; my windbreaker is admired by almost everyone. One soldier offered me $30 for it. But of course I would not sell, not at any price.

Thanks also for speaking to Tom Dolan. I know there would be no use speaking to him on Rotary Frolic night, but hope you can do it soon. I told the Stamps that I had asked you to speak to him. They think it is a very good idea and also said that if I could get back here after the war, they could introduce me to some well known foreign correspondents. Moo seemed to think journalism would be a good thing for me.

If this war goes on much longer, I will almost be able to live off the interest on my bonds! But I should save some ready cash, don't you think?

Love,

Tom

P.S. *Saturday morning*— I just heard that the talk about leave to Canada is a lot of hooey— propaganda, I guess. So we won't be able to count on that at all. Sorry.

— 1945 —

January 10

Dear Mom,

I don't know what the heck is wrong, but just the merest trickle of mail is getting through, and none of your letters have been in that trickle, which is very disappointing.

I hope everything is okay with you— in spite of the winter— which from all reports seems to be a hell-damner.

We have not been doing a thing this last week. A few days ago, I missed the chance to visit an ex-concentration camp. There is a possibility I may still see it, and I hope I can, even though it cannot be what anyone (with the possible exception of Huns) could call a pleasant sight.

The main thought amongst the soldiers at the moment is leave to England, and mine comes this month; I was lucky enough to have my name drawn first! Amazing. So in two weeks I shall cross the Channel again.

About leave to Canada— I would rather not talk about it— but here goes— they have a new system. First you need the five years of overseas service— which I have just got. That gives one 60 points— one per month. On top of that, there are six points for a wife in Canada and six points for each wound.

After that— which is quite fair and right— a measly few are

taken, so there is a waiting list a mile long of those who were eligible for the first draft.

January 11— We went over to see the farm family we were billeted with before. I was given my "clompes," or wooden shoes. I now have a small ornamental pair and a pair for wearing.

As soon as I can get a suitable box, I will send them home. Would you give one of the small ones to Phyl, when they arrive?

Today has been almost a holiday, with no patients so far; rather than stay in the clinic, which is either an ice house or a gas house, I am writing this in my "boudoir."

I haven't heard from Bob since before Christmas. Guess he is quite busy. According to the newspapers, the Canadians are doing all right in Italy. The going must be pretty tough, and having had a taste of what that means, I do not envy Bob. I hope above all that he is okay!

Keep your fingers crossed for victory...

Love,

Tom

January 22
Dear Mom,

I am glad, Mom, that you and Trix are feeling not so bad, considering the circumstances. I know what you mean when you say you are numb with shock. I was the same way when I heard the news. I didn't know what to think— let alone do or say.

Today I saw a very lovely and applicable thought. "We all must die some time— but we can't all die for something."

Mom, know that Bob did die for something, and it is up to us to make that something a reality. I have often heard the phrase, "We must not lose faith with those who have died," but it never meant as much to me as it does now. We have to keep going— stronger than ever.

I am so glad to hear that the neighbours and friends have been so good to you— that everyone has been so good. Knowing that one has friends in a time of need is a consolation.

I have started to work on a compassionate leave and then a reposting in Canada. I wish I could be with you now.

Goodnight and God bless you.

Love,
Tom

March 2
Dear Mom,

According to tonight's radio the Hun is beginning to cross the Rhine in an effort to get out of the trap. I hope he doesn't make it.

Our living conditions at the moment are quite good— warm and dry. But they may change at a moment's notice— so we are making the best of them.

There are quite a few civilians around— women and children only. They don't seem the least embarrassed or ashamed. In one way, I think the Germans are the most amazing people of the world. How anyone could be so stupid and yet so two-faced, so simple and yet so complex, I don't know.

They are certainly not individualists; they accept orders and regimentation that would make any red-blooded man boil. But they take all that for granted. Some of them try to be friendly, but the "No Fraternizing" order is well and willingly obeyed. In fact, I think many of the boys get itchy fingers whenever they see a German, civilian or not.

For all of Hitler's ranting, though, they have so far caused us no trouble at all. On the contrary, they seem quite happy. A few of the young girls still remain Nazis— according to stories— and still believe Germany will win the war. I have not seen any Nazi regalia on anyone myself; I am afraid that if I did, I would be up for murder.

Enough about this scourge of the earth.

Love,

Tom

March 7

Dear Mom,

My leave has been okayed from this end, so it is just a matter of time— but the army does take its time. Our Colonel could have hurried it a lot more than he did, but this is the first time he has had to do anything like this— and he didn't think I had a chance. He is not a very good man when it comes to looking after his men's interests— a shining example of why I have decided against dentistry. But we can talk all about that when we see each other. It is much easier to explain than to write.

Every time I see the Colonel now my heart stops beating until I have heard what he has to say.

With that one exception though, everyone has been most kind to me— Andy Johnson, the Colonel's Adjutant, and Captain Mackenzie. Between them, they made the matter a cinch. And even though it took longer having everything checked by them, it was much better than having the Dental Corps do the whole business and mess it up.

So glad to hear that Don did not mind about me "using" his health. That *was* most important— and the fact that he had already been discharged from the Army and the Air Force fitted in perfectly.

When I started the whole thing, the first question everyone asked was, "Have you any brothers in Canada?"

Cologne has fallen today— and tomorrow— who knows!

Our "home" is quite comfortable; we have a whole house and it is dry and fairly warm. But don't ever believe that the Huns were (or are) running short of food and the necessities of life. This house has so much furniture in it that there was no room to move, and lots of coal and evidence of lots of food.

There is a family living beside us and they are looking after the cows in our barn. They claim they are Russians. But if one believed all these stories, there were mostly Russians, Poles, Czechs, Dutch, and Belgians in Germany, and hardly any Germans.

They asked us if we wanted some milk— and we rudely told them "No." They are acting the same way as we heard they did after the last war. They have even asked some of our soldiers to spend the evening with them. Can you imagine such gall! They are ignored completely. And that is good.

Your suggestion of sending food instead of clothes to the Dutch is a very good one. They really need it. And I hate to think what the northern part of Holland is like.

Another thing they need urgently is medical supplies. It is impossible to get even iodine. The doctors have absolutely nothing— about all they can do is diagnose.

I went back to see the Haems last night. They are really pleasant and good people— and have definitely made up their mind to have at least a holiday in Canada— and they hope to be able to stay there. Frankly, I hope so, too. They are not very optimistic about conditions in Europe— and they are both really hard workers. That is something quite rare!

In the room now there are five men besides myself. The centre of interest is a sewing machine— which, after two hours, one of them has finally found out how to work. They are sewing a collar on a shirt— one sewing, and all the others giving instructions— "Watch your finger," "Keep her on the track," "Oh, Christ, thread's off the shuttle." It's really comical...

So long for now.

Love,

Tom

March 12

Dear Mom,

Thank you for the marmalade; my mouth is watering!

I'm glad to hear Harry is getting his discharge. I wish I could say the same thing.

Had some bad news from the Stamps today— Moo's mother has been bombed out. Luckily, everybody got out unhurt. But since they went through the whole Blitz, their nerves were none too good to start with, and I think Moo's mother must be pretty busted up.

The war is going exceptionally well— from the Generals' point of view. And the German people are suffering— not nearly enough— but they are suffering— and that is something.

Give my very best regards to Trix— and keep smiling.

Love,

Tom

April 22

Dear Mom,

This is the letter I have been waiting so long to write. Word came through yesterday afternoon just as we were preparing to move, so I could not write till today. I will be leaving here in about a week.

Looking forward, that week seems an age. But by the time you get this, I will be on my way home.

I don't know anything about the arrangements, but imagine it will take a month at least, and more likely a month-and-a-half, to make the journey. I left Canada June 11, 1940— and who knows, I might return the same day, five years later.

The thought of seeing Canada and coming home again gives me a feeling which is impossible to explain, like a long dream finally coming true. Sometimes I am frightened I will wake up and find it was only a dream.

Be seeing you soon!

Love,
Tom

May 11
Dear Mom,
I am in England, waiting for a boat. Under ordinary circumstances, I would probably have been on the ocean by now— but with all the P.O.W.s being released, we have to wait. They get top priority— which is as it should be. We should be leaving very soon— but don't expect to see me before the end of the month at the earliest. There is such an uproar that no one knows, from day to day, what is happening.

V.E. Day has come at last! It is a great feeling to know that there is no more war here— but hardly believable! Tuesday and Wednesday were declared holidays for practically the whole army. I met Moo with her stepfather at the station in London, and Moo and I had lunch before she went back home.

I waited to see Churchill at Downing Street and met a very nice lady who worked at the B.B.C. We joined forces, and finding out that Winnie was not likely to appear, we wandered through the crowds to the Palace. It was then about 8:30, so we got a good place and heard the King's speech broadcast from the loudspeakers set up all over. After the broadcast, the Royal Family, and Churchill, appeared on the balcony; it was quite a moving sight. There must have been 100,000 people there— all cheering madly.

From there, the B.B.C. girl and I went to hunt up a pub, which was very difficult; those that were open were jammed tight, and most of them had already sold out everything they had. We finally asked a middle-aged couple if they knew where there was a pub— and the lady replied, "What do you want? A drink or a bed?" It was very embarrassing, but they turned out to be nice people and invited us to their flat for a beer. Then the B.B.C. girl caught the last tube home, and I continued wandering— back to the Palace, which was all lit up, where I saw the King and Queen again— then to the West End— and finally to Trafalgar Square, where I slept for a few hours. Spent the next day at the Stamps'. After lunch, I was so tired I slept away the afternoon. I am so over-anxious, I can't settle down to anything.

Love,

Tom

Afterword

When the publishers, Bev and Don, presented me with the manuscript for this book, I was really overwhelmed. "These old letters— in a book!" I couldn't believe it.

I only wrote the letters; I had never read them until now.

But, I asked, wasn't there a letter about the Gestapo H.Q. in Antwerp? And how about my meeting with the unseen guard on the road east from Nijmegan?

"No," came the answer.

I realized that these events— and others from toward the end of the war— must have been described in letters that somehow went astray. Or perhaps I never did write home about them, because our regiment was moving so fast.

So here goes— a couple of "fill-ins" that stick out in my mind and that I hope will be interesting to the reader.

I think I was with the Essex Scottish at the time we went into Antwerp; whoever I was with, we were the troops liberating the city.

The first night there, a few of us decided to go into town. We got various rides that took us to a section of Antwerp comparable to Toronto's Yonge and Front Streets. Then we walked north on "Yonge." It was wild; it was night— and all the lights were on! That may sound silly, but after five years of blackout, this was a big moment.

I was with a group, I hate to say it, of really dull, boring Canadians. The bars were open; everything was open; and everybody was celebrating, drinking and dancing in the streets. The Germans were only a few blocks away, but everybody knew they were on the run.

I was ready to join in the celebrations, but my pals just kept gawking and saying, "You'd never see anything like this back home!"

We'd come to an "ice cream" place that didn't have real ice cream, but something like it that was close enough. In the streets around us, the dancing, the drinking, and the singing beckoned; but my pals crowded around the "ice cream" booth, saying, "Oh, boy!" We all had an ice cream and headed straight back to camp.

What could I do?

As we were on the way back— walking through a district that reminded me of Rosedale in Toronto— an older couple came out of a doorway and greeted us with tears in their eyes. We were the first "liberation troops" they had talked to— and they invited us in. My friends said, "We have to get back to camp."

So I said, "Can I visit you tomorrow night?"

The couple was delighted.

When I returned the following night, the Royal Carpet was laid out, beginning with a bath. This was supposed to be the best thing one could offer a soldier.

I was led to the bathroom and shown how to turn on the "heater." It was a small gas flame, almost enough to light a cigarette, underneath a huge iron tank.

The water was icy cold— but what could I do?

Anyway, after lots of conversation and the best food they had— plus cognac— they told me that the former Gestapo H.Q. was just up the street (naturally, in the best part of town) and that it had been taken over by the Belgian Underground.

So, on my way home, I wondered whether I could get in to see the H.Q. I must admit, it took some talking, but the guard, a Belgian Undergrounder come above ground, ushered me in. It was a plush-looking building— with pictures of the heroes of the Third

Reich still hanging— and then they asked me if I would like to see the prison cells.

I was led downstairs— the entry into one of the most scary experiences of my life. There was an open space, with maybe 15 or 20 people standing around— local collaborators who had been captured and imprisoned by the Underground— men in shirts with sleeves sliced off and trousers out at the knees. They were surrounded by cells crammed with women, who, when I was "exhibited" to them as an Allied soldier, spit on the few inches of ground that they did not occupy.

The men were being tortured. I had never seen anything like it and hope never to see such things again. It was not only disgusting, but humiliating that mankind could stoop so low.

In contrast was a humourous scene that took place in Holland, in a town called Malden, about five miles east of Nijmegan.

I had been getting more and more involved with the Haims— one of the most courageous couples I have ever met. They were, of course, with the Dutch Underground, which, after liberation, came out in the open.

After the war was over, the Dutch Underground, like most liberation movements, immediately arrested all collaborators and set up tribunals to judge them. It soon became obvious that the jails were so overcrowded that the situation was becoming impossible. So they reversed the system of justice; those who had been arrested were allowed the privilege of writing to the tribunal and explaining why they should be freed.

One night, the head of a tribunal— and leader of the Province of Gelderland Underground— came to the Haims', as he did frequently. He told this story:

Many of the so-called collaborators were young girls who,

because most of the Dutch men had been shipped off to labour camps, had cohabited with German soldiers. One of these girls wrote to the tribunal, admitting the charge against her, but explaining that in between the time of liberation and the time she had been arrested, she had slept with five Canadians, one Brit, and three Americans— so she was really an internationalist.

They immediately released her!

In the same Nijmegan salient another scary but comical scene took place.

Our headquarters had been moved from Malden to an even smaller village called Mook. Mook was almost on the German border, and our unit was in a holding pattern.

So I took off one night and returned to Malden, about three miles down the road, to visit the Haims. We had, as usual, a candlelight dinner (there was no power after 7 p.m.) using tidbits of food from packages from home, accompanied by wines and liqueurs and champagne which had been "liberated" on the way through northern Europe (it was a tough war!).

But at about 11 p.m., the sky was filled with the drone of planes, and then shelling started.

Something was up; I thought I'd best get back to my unit.

(I was right. It was the night Montgomery decided to make the big push into Germany.)

Since our troops were in the front line, other Allied troops were coming from the rear and leap-frogging over and around us. All Hell was breaking loose— bombers, fighters, artillery, and small arms fire. Remember, this was out on the Nijmegan salient, jutting almost into Germany and surrounded on all sides by what was left of the German army.

I was walking along the road in the pitch dark, trying to keep my courage up, when a voice from the ditch shouted something to me. I was taken aback— I still don't know what he said— but I realized it must be the password. Of course, I didn't know the answering password, but I recognized the accent of the man who spoke from the ditch as Canadian.

To get out of this situation, I decided to be a typical Canadian soldier (I still couldn't see the guy who was challenging me), so I said: "Jesus Christ, Mack, I don't know the fucking password." The voice responded, "You stupid son of a bitch— what the hell are you doing out tonight? Get back to your unit as soon as you can!"

I stayed in Holland only about a year, but it seemed that many of the most dramatic events took place there— maybe because the war was coming to a culmination and events were piling up on one another.

One of the most touching and poignant moments of the whole five years came in December of 1944. It was close to Christmas, and our unit had a Christmas party. It was like something out of a nineteenth-century story book. We were billeted on a farm and took over the barn— a one-storey, typical Dutch structure— still housing the cattle. One couldn't have designed a better nativity scene: there were animals, straw, and light... We were having a wonderful party, and then, to add to it, an old school friend from Stratford, Bob Johnston, arrived. The Perth Regiment had just arrived in Holland from Italy, and Bob had come over especially to see me.

Here we were, thousands of miles from home— still two home town boys. But he must have been shocked when he saw how happy I was.

He got me aside and said, "I was really sorry about your brother Bob." I looked at him in silence. He realized that, until then, I had not been notified that my brother had been killed a few days earlier.

I felt so sorry for Bob Johnston; he was mortified. Needless to say, the party took on a whole different perspective. It became the reality of life and death— and at Christmas, with the cattle lowing, in a barn.

We went from the Nijmegan salient away up to Gronigen in the very north of Holland, where we had the honour of liberating the city.

We happened to be in one of the better-class areas, but even then we had to sleep either in or under our trucks— until the locals saw the situation and invited us into their gracious homes. Of course, we brought food; I'll never forget our hosts' exclamations of surprise when we unwrapped a loaf of bread. The residents gathered around it and couldn't believe that it was actually white!

We didn't stay there long. We swung south again through Holland, took a sharp turn into Germany, and ended up in a small village on the road to Frankfurt.

It was here that I came into contact with my first concentration camp. It was Polish, and the freed ex-prisoners were walking around town proudly showing their "P" arm bands, which had so recently been signs of their condemnation.

I was only there a day or so when word came through that because my father had died, my brother had been killed in Italy, and because I had served five years overseas, I was being given compassionate leave to return to Canada.

Tom Patterson,
Toronto/Stratford
August, 1995

Editor's Note

TOM PATTERSON'S letters home from England and the Allied front were saved by his mother and remained carefully packaged for fifty years. The letters collected here represent only a fraction of those Tom Patterson wrote during this time; there were many more, to friends, to his sister and brothers, to individuals and organizations acting in support of the Canadian troops, and others, that are lost to us.

The letters published in *They Never Rationed Courage* were distilled from an original 500, and further edited. The names of some of the men with whom Tom Patterson served have been changed. Missing here are references to unpreserved letters, family in-jokes, gossip about mutual acquaintances, and other material that would have been a mystery to any reader not part of the Patterson household, but all further evidence of the love and esteem in which the family members held one another. Also excised were scores of thank-yous and appreciations of family kindnesses, lists that tracked parcels with reference numbers, and careful assessments and wonderings about how much time letters were taking to traverse the ocean in both directions.

They Never Rationed Courage provides a rare and honest record of wartime, of a family that pulled together through adversity, and of a kind of collective Canadian support for the war effort that seems almost unimaginable today. We therefore learn much from it, not only about historical events and individual courage, but about human possibility.

I would especially and particularly like to thank Tom Patterson, for his kindness and cooperation, and his wife, Pat Patterson, for her help and patience. Thanks also to Bruce Barber for keyboarding Tom Patterson's often faded but always elegant handwriting; and Lisa Brant of the Stratford Festival Archives for setting in motion the publication of this book. — *Beverley Daurio, Stratford, 1995*